MW01010557

THREADGILL'S

The Cookbook

THREADGILL'S

THE COOKBOOK

◆◆◆

BY EDDIE WILSON, PROPRIETOR

LONGSTREET PRESS
Atlanta, Georgia

Published by Longstreet Press, Inc.
A subsidiary of Cox Newspapers,
A subsidiary of Cox Enterprises, Inc.
2140 Newmarket Parkway, Suite 118
Marietta, Georgia 30067

Printed in the United States of America

First printing 1996

ISBN 1-56352-277-2
Library of Congress Card Catalog Number: 95-82241

All Threadgill's restaurant photographs by Andrew Yates, except where otherwise designated.

Cover illustration by Bill Narum.

Threadgill's Comic Book by Jack Jackson.

Illustration and design by Kevin Combs.

Art direction and book design by Ben Davis.

Media consultancy by Woody Roberts.

Electronic film prep and separations by Overflow Graphics Inc., Forest Park, GA

Special thanks to Becky Threadgill, who shared her Threadgill family photos.

Threadgill's · 6416 North Lamar · Austin, TX 78752
(512) 451-5440 · (800) 580-5040
http://www.threadgills.com

Beulah Risher Wilson, 1922–1986

My Momma never had a secret.

This book is dedicated to her memory.

CONTENTS

FOREWORD ix

ACKNOWLEDGMENTS xi

INTRODUCTION 1

1: SIXTY YEARS AND COUNTIN' 9

2: NOTES FROM A SOUTHERN KITCHEN 17

3: THE PANTRY 31

STOCKS Beef Stock ◆ Chicken Stock ◆ Turkey Stock Vegetable Stock 32

SOUTHERN SPICES Meat Seasoning ◆ Poultry Seasoning Vegetable Seasoning ◆ Seafood Seasoning ◆ BBQ Rub 37

SAUCES, DRESSINGS AND SUCH Mayonnaise ◆ Lemon (or Lime) Mayonnaise ◆ Blue Cheese Dressing ◆ Hot Bacon Dressing for Spinach Salad Jalapeño Honey Mustard ◆ Vinegar and Oil ◆ Thousand Island ◆ BBQ Sauce Creole Sauce ◆ Chipotle Cream Sauce ◆ Cocktail Sauce ◆ Jezebel Sauce Pastalaya Base ◆ Citrus Butter ◆ Tartar Sauce ◆ Horseradish Sour Cream Sauce ◆ Smoked Corn Relish 40

GRAVIES Turkey Gravy ◆ Cream Gravy ◆ Skillet Cream Gravy Brown Gravy 51

4: THE MENU 55

SOUPS Cream of Broccoli Soup ◆ Vegetable Soup ◆ Tomato Soup Corn Soup ◆ Drunken Bean Soup ◆ Split Pea and Ham Soup ◆ Tortilla Soup ◆ Black Bean Soup ◆ Cold Tomatillo Soup 57

SALADS Carrot and Raisin Salad ◆ Broccoli/Cauliflower Salad ◆ Coleslaw Cottage Cheese and Cucumber ◆ French Quarter Pasta Salad ◆ Green Bean Salad ◆ Texas Caviar ◆ Potato Salad ◆ Ambrosia ◆ Cherry Cola Jell-O 63

BREADS Southern Cornbread ◆ Jalapeño Corn Muffins ◆ Aunt Onie's White Soda Cornbread ◆ Cornbread Dressing ◆ Threadgill's Biscuit Mix ◆ Buttermilk Biscuits ◆ Yeast Rolls ◆ Homestyle White Bread ◆ Whole Wheat Bread 71

EAT YOUR VEGETABLES! Mashed Potatoes ◆ New Potatoes with Garlic and Green Beans ◆ Scalloped Potatoes ◆ Yams or Sweet Potatoes Baked or Mashed ◆ Candied Sweet Potatoes ◆ Onions, Celery and Garlic ◆ Santa Fe Succotash ◆ Black-eyed Peas ◆ Hopping John ◆ Fresh Peas ◆ Baked Beans Green Beans ◆ Old South Butter Beans ◆ Red Beans and Rice ◆ Texas Chili Beans ◆ Refried Beans ◆ Snap Peas, Peppers and Corn ◆ Boiled Greens

Broccoli ◆ Cabbage ◆ Creole Cabbage ◆ Carrots ◆ Buttered Carrots Roasting Ears ◆ Sweet Corn Off the Cob ◆ Creamed Corn Diablo ◆ Garlic Cheese Grits ◆ Eggplant ◆ Cajun-Italian Eggplant ◆ Okra ◆ Stewed Okra and Tomatoes ◆ Yellow Squash ◆ Broccoli and Rice Casserole ◆ San Antonio Squash Casserole ◆ Spinach Casserole ◆ Spinach Casserole Bill Arnold Macaroni and Cheese ◆ Vegetarian Jambalaya 82

ENTRÉES AND VALUE MEALS 113

FRY IT IN THE SKILLET OR GRILL IT Chicken-Fried Steak and Cream Gravy ◆ Fried Chicken ◆ Fried Catfish ◆ Fried Oysters Catfish Moutarde ◆ Grillades and Grits ◆ Pork Stroganoff ◆ Tenderloin Jambalaya ◆ Seafood Pastalaya ◆ Chicken Pastalaya ◆ Vegetable Pastalaya Beef Liver with Onions ◆ Bronzed Catfish, Chicken Breast or Sirloin Steak Southwest Pork Chops ◆ Smoked Chicken Pasta Salad ◆ Bronzed Sirloin Pasta Salad 116

OVEN FOODS Meatloaf ◆ Glazed Ham with Jezebel Sauce Nashville Meatloaf ◆ Smothered Pork Chops ◆ French Quarter Catfish Seafood Jambalaya ◆ Spinach and Oyster Pie ◆ Stuffed Trout Spinach Pizza ◆ Chicken Enchiladas ◆ Salsa Verde 130

POT FOODS Chicken and Dumplings ◆ Beef Stew ◆ Pot Roast Texas Red Chili ◆ Mumbo-Gumbo 137

STEAKS 142

PORK AND HAM 143

SANDWICHES AND PICNICS B.L.T. ◆ Grilled Ham and Cheese Hot Roast Beef Sandwich ◆ Chicken Salad Sandwich 144

DESSERTS Pie Crust ◆ Pecan Pie ◆ Banana Pudding ◆ Salty Cracker Pie Mississippi Mud Cake ◆ Peach Cobbler ◆ Apple Pie ◆ Buttermilk Pie Double Chocolate Ice Box Pie ◆ Chocolate Brandy Cream ◆ Pumpkin Pie Strawberry Shortcake ◆ Sweet Potato Honey Pie ◆ Whipped Cream Chocolate Chip Cookies ◆ Vanilla Ice Cream ◆ Strawberry-Rhubarb Pie 153

BREAKFAST Fig Preserves ◆ Migas ◆ Breakfast Tacos ◆ Mock Hash Brown Potatoes ◆ Spinach Omelets ◆ Eggs Florentine 168

HOLD'JA OVERS AND SPIRITUALS Bloody Mary ◆ Threadgill's Margarita ◆ Pitcher of Threadgill's Margaritas ◆ Armadillo World Headquarters Nachos ◆ Fried Green Tomatoes ◆ Chile con Queso ◆ Chicken-Fried Strips (Chicken or Beef) ◆ Fried Chicken Livers ◆ Stuffed Mushroom Caps Stuffed Jalapeños 174

THE COMIC BOOK 189

THE SCRAPBOOK 214

THE BOOK SEARCH 231

REDEDICATION 237

INDEX 238

THANKS TO THREADGILL'S

THE DIFFICULTY in describing a beautiful song, a favorite city, a great movie or anything personally favored is that blatant, obvious factors get equal billing with the subtle and invisible. The description falters and you are left with urging the practical alternative: "You just have to go there and find out for yourself!"

Austin, Texas, is a phenomenon that I am unable to describe satisfactorily. There are lakes and trees, the beautiful hill country, ethnic diversity, Texas hospitality, and on and on.... But more than all that, there is a certain pervasive attitude, unspoken but virtually unanimous, that things like music and fun and food (and their enjoyment!) are important. That they are at least equally as important as politics, fashion, status and maybe even more so. (If I am just projecting, then so much the better for me!)

Music and friends first lured me to Austin. It was in the late '60s, and among my earliest memories of it there stands out a night of what almost seemed like a homecoming. At the suggestion of T. J. McFarland, a small group of us headed out to "some beer joint on North Lamar." There we heard Kenneth Threadgill and Bill Neely playing some of the best music I have heard yet. The room was filled with just about every shade of local color: hippies, rednecks, politicians, college kids (and professors, probably). Wisecracks and laughter filled the spots between songs. At some point John Reed and I even got up and played a couple of tunes. Little did I know how many evenings I would eventually spend in that place, and with how many friends, laughing and singing.

The story continued with the advent of the Armadillo World Headquarters, where Eddie Wilson managed to harness enough of this peculiar energy to create one of the most spectacularly successful failures (for about 10 years!) that I know of. I missed a lot of it, but I was there for the first night, the last night and a lot of good ones in between. The world kept spinning, and Eddie decided on a slightly different approach. He scaled it down, went north (on Lamar), took over an old friend's business, made the food the focus, and it added up to a wonderfully successful success.

Music took care of itself, eventually, because Kenneth (Mr. Threadgill, that is) couldn't stay away. The Wednesday night jams were uniformly wonderful and the food was great on any day of the week. For those reasons I was there quite often, and there was one other important reason. Janet Branch, the girl whom I would eventually marry, was a waitress there.

After Kenneth's voice became too weak, the traditional Wednesday night music at Threadgill's was silenced for a while. But in February 1988, Eddie suggested the best way to celebrate the release of my first album on Hightone Records was by having a party at Threadgill's. It turned out so well that he and my manager, Mike Crowley, decided it was worth a try to see if we could duplicate it the next week. That started a three-year run during which I, with the help of Roger Polson and Champ Hood, hosted a weekly jam session that saw a virtual Who's Who of the Texas (and beyond) music world perform for virtually no money but for better food and more fun than anyone can buy. The Wednesday night Sittin' and Singin' and Supper Sessions continue at Threadgill's, and the good food continues every day. And I am happy to tell you, that invisible magic I felt the first time I was there is still alive. Still alive in Austin, still alive at Threadgill's, and especially still alive in the hearts of all the talented people involved in bringing you this more-than-a-cookbook.

—Jimmie Dale Gilmore
from Spicewood, Texas
Easter Sunday, April 7, 1996

Acknowledgments

THE JOB OF THANKING EVERYONE who helped with this book has caused me nightmares. In one, I am the pitiful soul on stage at an awards ceremony, thanking everyone under the sun. I'm nervous, stammering, desperately trying to remember every last dear, important person in my life, clinging to the microphone, knowing I've taken too long but there are many more to thank. Then someone calls out from the audience, "Don't use my name in that awful little book!" Someone else yells, "Get down! You've won no award!" Of course, I wake up in a sweat.

In another dream, all is going well. The book is out at last. I have thanked everyone under the sun. Life is sweet. I'm walking into the Quik Print to pick up some ... oh, my God, I forgot to thank Bill and his crew for all their help. Good honk! I'm not even going to begin a list. You know who you are and even if you have a doubt, I certainly don't.

Not a Lobster Taco

For my rallying cry I must credit Dean Fearing. In his beautiful *Mansion on Turtle Creek* cookbook, he explains what influences converged to enable him to make his mark on the Southwest, and uses as an example of that mark his wildly popular lobster taco. At the end of his explanation he states, "And once you've tried a Lobster Taco, you'll know it is not 'everyday' food." Eureka! There at last was my cuisine defined: Everyday food. Three hundred sixty-five days a year we serve food that we hope is perfect for a large part of our neighborhood to eat every day. I think you will agree that once you have tasted the Threadgill's Meatloaf, you will know it is not a lobster taco.

✌ Come see me when you're hungry!

— Eddie Wilson (A.K.A. Austin Blackie)

Howdy
STRANGER
TV, Comics&More

Introduction

I GUESS THERE'S NO PUTTING THIS OFF. I've been collecting the stuff for this little book for a lotta years and now I've finally got to slap it between the covers. Longstreet is on the phone and they say the printer is holding up the presses. So here goes. But before I get started, you should be forewarned that I have a tendency to ramble just a little. And to make matters worse, this story has a lot of strange tangents and subplots. To try and make matters better I've added a bunch of show and tell.

First of all, I need to say a word about show and tell. When I was young I didn't have a clue about what to be when I grew up. I always aimed at doing something with my life that would be worth a book. I knew early on that it would not be a book about rocket science but I did know that it would have a dust cover that would briefly list my accomplishments. Though I didn't even try to imagine what all that list might include (rodeo clown, lawyer, soldier, inventor, coach, poet, peacemaker, private eye), I always wanted to make one claim to fame regardless of what else I did or didn't make out of my life. I wanted my dust jacket to proudly state that E.O.W. was one heck of a short order cook. When I was still a college freshman, I came upon a little book of short stories titled *Southern Fried* that drove deeper this desire. Its title story was about a philosophical short order cook and a showboating soda jerk. They had a late-night showdown of Olympic proportions and the simple moral was that planning and grace, though seemingly slow at times, almost always outdistance flamboyance and wasted motion in the end. I couldn't get any of my college profs to read *Southern Fried*. Perhaps because it was illustrated by Jack Davis, the *Mad* magazine cartoonist, they wouldn't take it seriously. So I studied my American Naturalists and the British Empiricists and the Existentialists and dropped out of school. I decided not to go to law school and not to become a teacher and not to go into advertising. I was a bust as a beatnik poet, fired as a high school coach and bored nearly to death as a junior lobbyist trainee for the Texas Division of the United States Brewer's Association. So I became a hippie promoter of the arts until the pressures nearly drove me crazy. That's when I finally made my leap. I rented a 32-seat dump and named it the Raw Deal. I became a short order cook and amateur historian of the neighborhood. I've lived a well-fed cartoon life of music and art ever since.

As most of Threadgill's Wednesday Night Supper session regulars know by now, I am a recovering Shy Person. The most successful part of my therapy has involved wearing a garish vegetable suit, reciting from Guy Clark's and Roy Blount's food songs on stage at our Wednesday night Sittin', Singin' and Supper sessions. The troubadours provide a bit of lilt so that I don't freeze up and stammer to a stop. Sprinkled through this book are a few of my favorite lines. Also, to help me over my self-consciousness at having no experience as a writer, I've enlisted Jack Jackson to tell this history in comic-book form. Jack is not only recognized by Texas scholars as one of the state's finest historians, but he actually created the genre called underground comics in 1964 with a publication called *God Nose*. He was a close friend of Janis Joplin and the regular tape recorder operator at the Wednesday night hootenanny performances at Threadgill's in the early '60s when she was performing there.

> ◆
>
> Threadgill's Restaurant is not only known for my mother's Southern cooking, it's also a museum of Austin music history and a shrine to its founder, the Grandfather of Austin Country Music, Kenneth Threadgill.
>
> ◆

A remarkable artist and cook, Kevin Combs has contributed the wonderful illustrations of items from my collection, and considerable design guidance for the book. His love for this project has touched every aspect, from the food to the music to the feel. He has shaped my show and tell so that you can figure out where this story is happening as you read along. Burton Wilson, famed photo-chronicler of Austin blues and rock-and-roll in the '60s and '70s, is a daily example of good taste around the restaurant. As always, everything I've ever done is largely the result of help from my friends.

Threadgill's Restaurant is not only known for my mother's Southern cooking, it's also a museum of Austin music history and a shrine to its founder, the Grandfather of Austin Country Music, Kenneth Threadgill. If it seems like my mother's Southern cooking, frozen spinach casserole, an old Austin gas station with art gallery, and the singing career of Janis Joplin don't have much to do with each other at first, please bear with me. Eventually all these subjects will wind up telling the story of how a humble little American family restaurant grew up to feed millions of happy customers. And I guarantee that you'll also get some good eating out of the deal if you're patient enough.

I guess the best way to explain all this is just to treat you like any other honored guest who comes to visit Threadgill's. I'll take you for a little tour of the "Joint" and the little museum of historical curiosities I call the "Upstairs Store." We'll look at my collection of old photos and family mementos. I'll show you my collection of old kitchen equipment and cooking devices. After you peruse my library of comic books, then I'll stuff you with down-home Southern cooking. But since you can't actually sit down and eat, I'll just give you the recipes and let you cook the food yourself. Mother would be proud.

The tour begins today right here at the house. This is where my wife Sandra and I keep the archives that aren't hanging on the walls for the public to view. Our library consists mainly of cookbooks, gardening books, and Austin history in many forms. We live right behind the commissary, smack-dab in the middle of town. When Kenneth began his little family business here, this neighborhood was a couple of miles north of the Austin city limits. There were pens for chickens and hogs behind the station, and a few cows. Before WWII was very old, local realtors were advertising lots in this area as being large enough to build a home and have room left over for a Victory Garden to grow vegetables for the family. One-hundred-dollar lots for 20 dollars down and 50 cents a week.

From our front porch it's a slow half-minute walk through the garden to the commissary behind Threadgill's. We've got a guard cat that keeps most of the birds out of Sandra's garden and a few birds that keep out most of the bugs. We've got good bugs that eat the bad bugs and the good bugs are rewarded with the best compost in the world from all the vegetable trimmings out of the commissary across the street.

The Threadgill's complex includes the restaurant and the two-story commissary out back of the parking lot. Between them and my

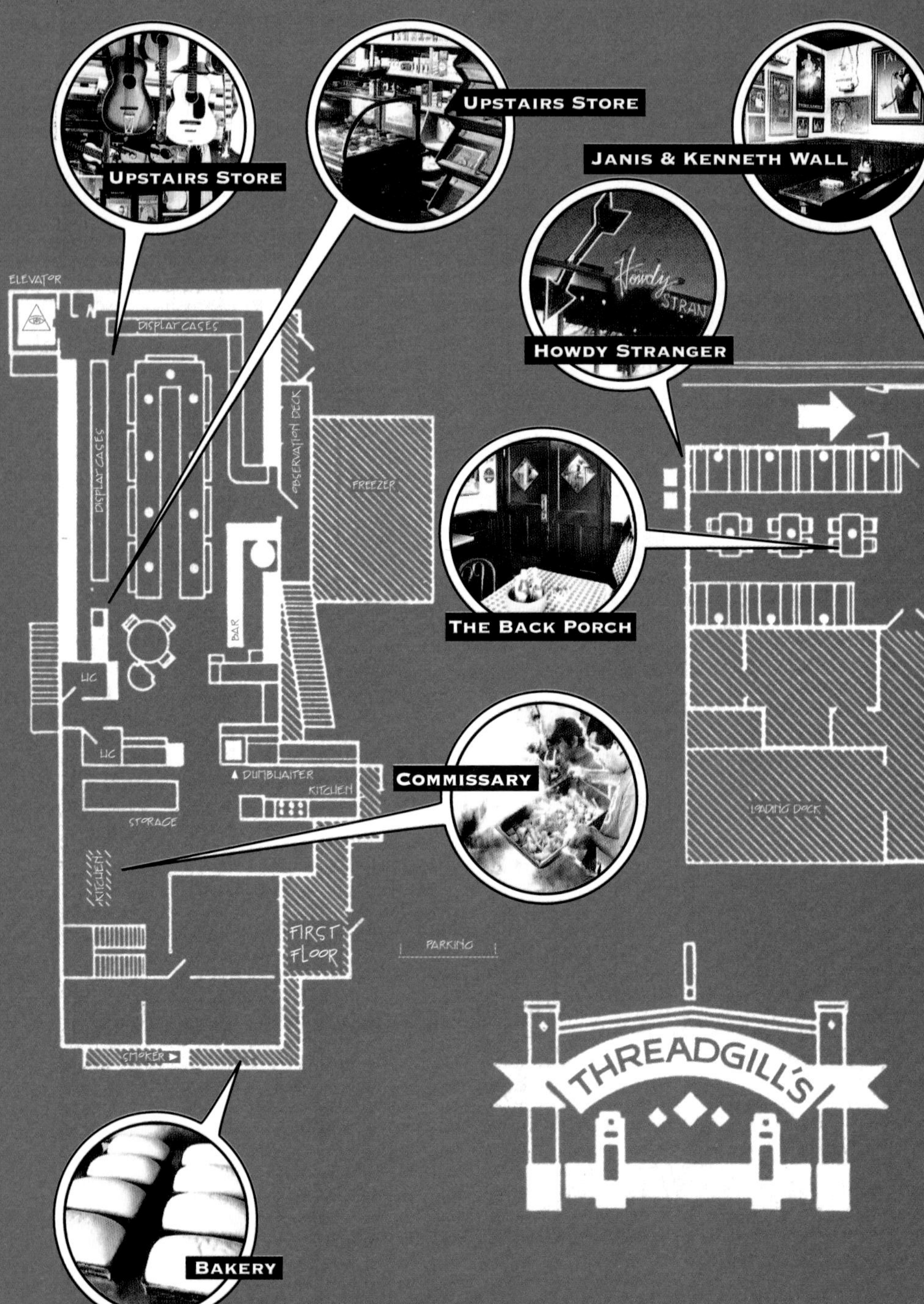
Upstairs Store
Upstairs Store
Janis & Kenneth Wall
Howdy Stranger
The Back Porch
Commissary
Bakery
ELEVATOR
DISPLAY CASES
DISPLAY CASES
OBSERVATION DECK
FREEZER
BAR
LIC
LIC
DUMBWAITER
KITCHEN
STORAGE
KITCHEN
FIRST FLOOR
PARKING
SMOKER
LOADING DOCK
THREADGILL'S

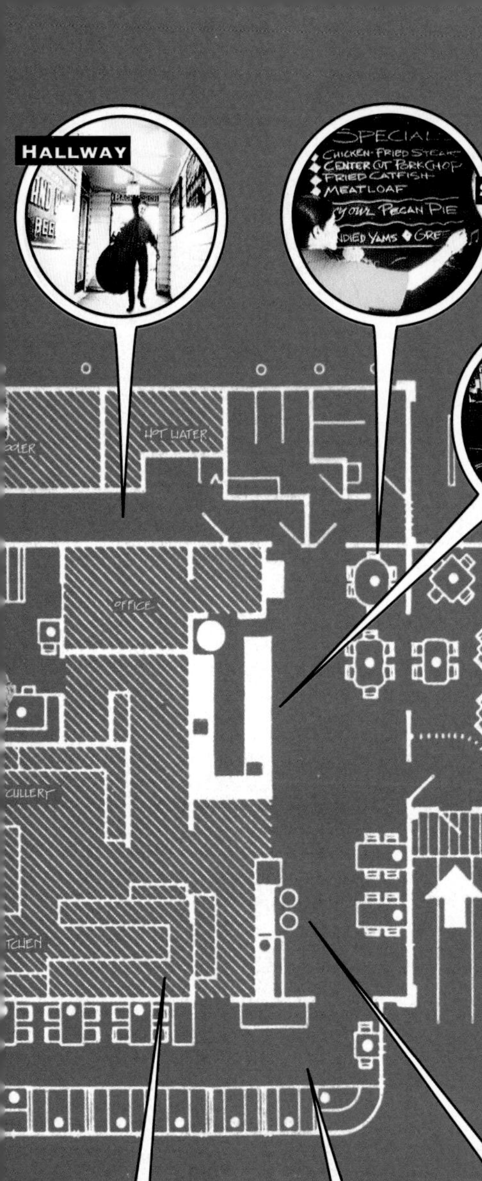

Hallway

Specials Board

Stage

Bar

Front Room

Front Entrance

Kitchen

Diner

To-Go Counter

house there are five kitchens, five porches, two gardens, two lunch counters, a bar and the "Upstairs Store." I call it that because Threadgill's Country Store Museum and Banquet Hall is too long a name for me to remember, even on a good day. In addition to the bakery and the blast freezer that makes ours so different from most restaurant kitchens, the commissary is kinda proud of an unusual assortment of extra-large cooking equipment. It's got 10 ovens, a potato peeler that'll peel 50 pounds of spuds in five minutes, a couple of 60-gallon kettles, three 30-gallon braising pans that tilt for easy pouring and a smoker that'll hold 600 pounds of meat. Our huge menu is labor-intensive and would not be possible without the commissary. On an average day we serve about 700 pounds of mashed potatoes and 50 gallons of gravy.

A quick glance around the restaurant itself usually generates a lot of questions from newcomers. Like: "Why are there gas pumps out front?" "Why are there so many pictures of Janis Joplin on the walls?" "Where did the records on this funky jukebox come from?" So after a stroll through the restaurant and a cold beer at the bar or a cup of coffee at our little two-stool lunch counter, I usually answer these questions by bringing my visitors to the Upstairs Store.

◆

> A quick glance around the restaurant usually generates a lot of questions from newcomers. I usually answer these questions by bringing my visitors to the Upstairs Store.

◆

Over the years, I've been asked so many questions about my Armadillo World Headquarters days and Mr. Threadgill's status as Grandfather of Austin Country Music, that I put my collection of photos and records and other music memorabilia on display. And since Janis Joplin was such a big part of the Threadgill's story, I've ended up with a few old artifacts from the Haight-Ashbury era too. A bunch of the '60s gang from Threadgill's went to San Francisco about the same time Janis did, and they produced poster art, comic books and cultural lore galore. I've saved some of the best bits and pieces.

A few years ago, when I began to sell Threadgill's frozen vegetable casseroles in stores around Texas, I really fell in love with the grocery business. My interest in old general

Photo: Eddie Wilson

THE UPSTAIRS STORE serves as both a banquet facility and country store museum.

stores intensified and their artifacts just seemed to find me. I became more passionate about American food and cooking. I began to find old cookbooks, kitchen utensils and food-processing gadgets from bygone days. I added them to the collection of cooking ephemera that Mother left me, and my display cases really began to swell with American kitchen history.

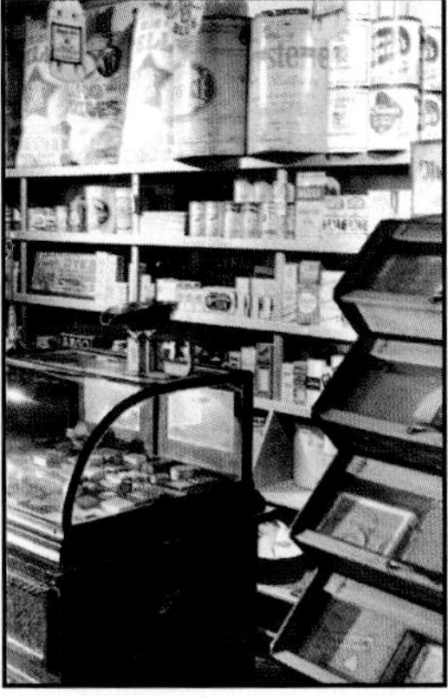

I hope to grow old up here doing little more than cooking for friends, collecting and sharing yarns, planning picnics and fishing trips and sitting around the store. I've gone and got too old to achieve my goal of being the titled "Prince of Picnic," so I guess I'll settle for being a "Senior Porch Person." I figure the word "store" must somehow be at the root of "storytelling." And I've always been partial to both.

Square One is a little dining room just off the back porch where we keep alive a tradition of oral history. It's part shrine to Kenneth and Janis and it's my favorite place to listen to old-timers tell tales about the neighborhood in the old days.

If you look over a few of these old photos, illustrations, comic strips and illustrations of kitchen tools in the book, I figure you can get a multimedia course in the history of Threadgill's. The next chapter gives a little running commentary with a time line that might explain a few things and give you a reference to help you untwist our chronology.

Pearl
THREADGILL

Chapter One

Sixty Years and Countin'

1933 WAS A KEY YEAR and a good place to start this little movie. Willie Nelson and Ann Richards were born. Jimmie Rodgers died. He was the first superstar of country music and Kenneth Threadgill's lifelong idol. That was also the year that my grandmother got a job as the welfare agent in Lumberton, Mississippi, and turned the cooking chores of the family's big farm kitchen over to my mother, Beulah, who was then 11 years old. Neither one of them had likely heard of Clarence Birdseye yet, but he was three years into his new effort to put frozen foods into American grocery stores.

It was also in **'33** that 22-year-old country music lover and enterprising bootlegger Kenneth Threadgill opened a Gulf gas station on what was then known as the Dallas Highway just north of the Austin city limits. After the county voted to "go wet" that year, Kenneth stood in line all night to be the first to get a beer license. Travis County Beer License #01, issued on **December 6, 1933**, belonged to Threadgill for the next 40 years.

In **1935**, Threadgill's gas station and beer joint was open 24 hours a day and gaining fame as an after-hours joint. Musicians working the dance-hall circuit hung out here for late-night gambling and jam sessions. In **1942**, a curfew was enacted and Kenneth Threadgill finally had to get a key for the front door; the place had never been locked before.

In **1943**, I was born in Lumberton, Mississippi. My momma had already been practicing the fine art of Southern cooking for 10 years. Threadgill's went through a slow period during World War II while Kenneth worked for the Corps of Engineers.

In **1948**, the city limits jumped north and Threadgill's became part of Austin. Kenneth Threadgill gave up on selling gas and Threadgill's became strictly a beer joint. In the evenings, Kenneth entertained the crowd with his renditions of songs by Jimmie Rodgers, "The Blue Yodeler." Kenneth had met Mr. Rodgers once when he

Photo: Threadgill's Archives

KENNETH THREADGILL

was performing at the Loew's Theatre in Houston, where Kenneth worked as an usher. Kenneth spent the rest of his life singing Rodgers's songs. It was the yodeling that got the Wednesday night singing sessions started at Threadgill's. Kenneth sang and yodeled and other musicians showed up with their instruments and joined in or played their own songs. The musicians were paid in beer.

In **1949**, my dad, Woody Wilson, moved our family to Austin when he joined the Austin Plumbers' Local. Beulah got her teaching certificate from the University of Texas while I climbed on the statues and fed the pigeons. She decided against teaching, though. She wanted to know just where I was as soon as school let out every day so she hung her diploma on the wall and opened a day nursery school. She and Woody built a big house on Avenue B in Hyde Park in **1954**, where she set up a nursery school built around the kitchen and started cooking lunch for 50 little kids every day. Maybe I ended up in the restaurant business because I was impressed with how happy she made people with her food.

It was around **1959** when I met Dottie Threadgill, Kenneth's daughter, while we were both at McCallum High School. She invited me to come out to the joint sometime and I took her up on the invitation. I was more interested in Dottie than in beer and country music when I visited Threadgill's the first time, but I never once found her there. I was impressed by how nice Mr. Threadgill was to me and I enjoyed visiting him. I would sit at the lunch counter nibbling on cheese and crackers and he would play records for me and tell me stories about the musicians who were playing. In **1961**, I enrolled in summer sessions at UT and it turned out that my English teacher, Stan Alexander, played country music with a few of his friends at Threadgill's every Wednesday night.

In **1962**, Janis Joplin enrolled at UT and fell in with a crowd of folkies. In those days, folkies were still somewhere in between beatniks and hippies, but they were immediate disciples of Mr. Threadgill and Stan's rural country blues. Once a week, this gang descended on the Texas Union at UT to drink beer and sing. The sessions got unsightly and in **1963**, the University banned beer drinking in the Union, no doubt partly to get rid of this bunch of undesirables.

So the longhaired crowd decided to venture into Threadgill's for a Wednesday night singing session—a brave move given the general attitude about hippies, beatniks and longhaired men among the rednecks of the era. But as he did with anybody else carrying an instrument, Kenneth Threadgill welcomed them with open arms and gave them free beer. Mr. Threadgill's kindness and tolerance and love for music had a calming effect on even the nastiest of the rednecks. Janis Joplin sang along to her autoharp accompaniment and started to develop her outrageous vocal style. When Mance Lipscomb was brought to perform at Threadgill's by the young folkies, the color barrier was broken in North Austin. Kenneth and his wife Mildred took a real interest in Janis and helped her through some tough times. By now I was among the Wednesday night regulars at Threadgill's.

I dropped out of college in **1964** and wandered around Mexico looking for Timothy Leary. When I got back, Kenneth had taken up his own musical career playing with a group called the Hootenanny Hoots. His little joint had been hassled by the fire department for having too many people in too small a place and it had become impossible to check the IDs of all the underage college students. Wednesday evenings had lost their charm for Kenneth and he shut down the Wednesday night hootenanny sessions. The Hoots played a country honky-tonk called the Split Rail for a couple of hundred Sunday nights in a row. Meanwhile, Janis had hitchhiked to San Francisco to check out the Haight-Ashbury love-in scene.

A whole lot of musical excitement exploded in the next 10 years. In **1965**, Jimmie Dale Gilmore came to

Photo: Larry Murphy

KENNETH THREADGILL WITH EDDIE WILSON, circa 1984

Austin and started playing occasionally at Threadgill's. In **1967**, Janis appeared with Big Brother and the Holding Company at the Monterey Pop Festival. In **1968**, Kenneth and the Hootenanny Hoots played the Newport Folk Festival. In **1970**, Janis had just released the *Pearl* album when she canceled a concert in Hawaii to fly back to Austin and make an appearance at a tribute and jamboree for Kenneth Threadgill.

At that time, I was talked into getting in the music business myself by managing a band called Shiva's Headband. But the Vulcan Gas Company, a club on Congress Avenue that had been the home of Austin's early hippie fringe, went out of business around then, so my band didn't have any place in Austin to play. That was when I got the bright idea of turning an empty old national guard armory south of the river into a music hall. So on **August 7, 1970**, we opened The Armadillo World Headquarters on $525\frac{1}{2}$ Barton Springs Road behind the Skating Palace.

Artist extraordinaire Jim Franklin's underground comic-style illustrations had already turned the armadillo into something of a mascot for Austin freaks, so the name was a natural and, of course, Jim Franklin became our resident graphic artist. His enormous murals and posters gave the place its unique Austin flavor.

October 1970. Austin went into mourning when we learned that Janis had died of a drug overdose.

September 1971. Without thinking to ask the landlord we tore out the offices of the armory and doubled the seating capacity of the Armadillo. This increased tenfold our capacity to lose money. I began to learn the new math of rock-and-roll.

Over the years, Armadillo World Headquarters added a kitchen and beer garden and I learned about nachos and guacamole. Among the kitchen employees I met were my first die-hard vegheads, and though I didn't understand them I learned quickly that many of the touring acts were as attracted to the food offered at the Armadillo as others were to our wildly vocal audience. Meanwhile we were booking acts like Bruce Springsteen, Jimmy Cliff, Frank Zappa, Van Morrison, Taj Mahal, and Bette Midler, as well as hosting theater and ballet and more and more country music.

Kenneth Threadgill played at Armadillo World Headquarters a lot. By now Kenneth had grown his hair long and had been to Nashville to record with Kris Kristofferson. Because of Kenneth's special place in the hearts of Austin music lovers, a lot of hippies developed an interest in country music. Of course, this unlikely redneck-hippie truce really traced its roots all the way back to the days when Janis Joplin and her folkies started sharing the stage with hillbilly bands at Threadgill's, but in **1972** something remarkable started happening.

That was the year that we booked Willie Nelson to play at the Armadillo. Willie and some of his friends weren't very happy with the Nashville country music establishment anyway, and being a Texas native and an outcast, Willie was in heaven here. Pretty soon the rebel country-and-western crowd had sort of blended in with the Armadillo World Headquarters hippie spirit, and Austin became the capital of the "Cosmic Cowboy" movement. We called them "headnecks in cowboy hats."

In **1974**, Kenneth's wife Mildred died, and Kenneth closed Threadgill's. The city of Austin almost had the place demolished because it had become an eyesore. Meanwhile, I had gotten pretty weary of the constant financial strain of trying to run Armadillo World Headquarters. In **1976**, I left it to start a hole-in-the-wall restaurant on Sabine Street called the Raw Deal. I was intrigued by the whole idea of a Southern cooking-style restaurant serving really honest food like my momma used to make.

It was time to earn my stripes as a short order cook. Ann Richards took the oath of office for her first elected job as County Commissioner at the Raw Deal on **January 1, 1977**. It was fun while it lasted, but the place wasn't really big enough to make a living.

I wanted to try the Southern cooking thing on a bigger scale, so in **1979**, I bought the deserted Threadgill's from Kenneth. The place had been gutted by a fire and needed a whole lot of work, but with Kenneth's encouragement, I dug in and started restoring the place. Almost two years later, Armadillo World Headquarters closed its doors on **New Year's Eve, 1980**. The next day, **January 1, 1981**, Threadgill's opened for business as a restaurant.

Maybe it was because the food was so good, maybe it was the history of the building, maybe it was the overflowing plates and the low prices, or maybe it was because we had the best waitresses in the city—I don't know why exactly—but Threadgill's was an instant hit. I didn't know what I was doing. I just held on for dear life. It would be foolish to overlook the possibility that some of the success stemmed from the thousands upon thousands of meals eaten over the years at Beulah's nursery school right down the street. During the first several years I spent greeting customers at the front door and the bar of the restaurant, I became reacquainted with dozens of professionals whose diapers I had changed in the '50s and early '60s.

Kenneth sang on Wednesday nights, just like in the old days. We added a stainless steel diner to handle the overflow crowds. In **1982**, a fire destroyed a lot of the building and I had to borrow more money to rebuild. Three months later we reopened, this time with a commissary kitchen and banquet hall. The banquet hall slowly evolved into the Country Store Museum and Eddie Wilson Memory Archive—the Upstairs Store.

In **1986**, stories about Threadgill's began to appear just about everywhere. A diner resurgence took hold, and everywhere you looked there was our picture: in *Newsweek*, *Rolling Stone*, *Smithsonian*, *National Geographic*, *Vogue*.

Beulah Wilson passed away on **September 1, 1986**. Kenneth Threadgill passed away on **March 20, 1987**.

On **September 12, 1987**, Kenneth Threadgill's birthday, Threadgill's hosted the first annual Austin Musicians' Appreciation Supper, where any musician in the city could eat free. In **1988**, Jimmie Dale Gilmore revived the old Wednesday night music tradition, now called the Sittin', Singin' and Supper Sessions.

In **1989**, Threadgill's frozen food operations got going. We started selling our chubs of spinach, beans

THREADGILL'S RESTAURANT, circa 1996

and rice, and San Antonio Squash to grocery stores all over Texas.

In **1993**, Threadgill's, Willie Nelson and Texas Governor Ann Richards all celebrated their 60th birthdays. Janis Joplin would have been 50 years old in 1993. I wish she could have been here for the party. As part of our oral history efforts we began an old-timers' reunion.

The story got goofier in **1994**. The Visa Card folks shot a commercial at Threadgill's just 'cause we don't take, have never taken, never intend to take American Express cards. Nothing personal, AmEx; it just never seemed like a good idea. But sure enough, it turned out to be a good idea not to. People all over the U.S. got a chance to glimpse for a few seconds, over and over again, our pretty customers, our huge portions and how much fun we have. *Gourmet* magazine printed a nice story about how good our food is and then *Bon Appétit* did something similar. Austin got real hot again and people started moving here so fast it looked for a while like all the U-Haul trucks and trailers in the world were gathering for a big party.

But ... you get the picture. Threadgill's isn't just a famous Southern-style restaurant. It's also a shrine to Kenneth Threadgill, the Father of the Austin music scene, and to Armadillo World Headquarters and country music and blues and to all the music and art that makes Austin a must-see place to visit.

By now I'm willing to bet that you're getting a little hungry. I promised that if you were patient you'd get some food out of this deal, so let's put the pictures away till after supper and wander over to the kitchen and see what's cooking.

THREADGILL'S
"GIVE PEAS A CHANCE."
THREADGILL'S

Chapter Two

Notes from a Southern Kitchen

THREADGILL'S IS A MUSEUM in more ways than one. Besides the photos and artifacts that tell the history of the joint, Threadgill's is also a museum of everyday Southern food the way Momma used to make it. I started the menu here at Threadgill's with a very deliberate attempt to preserve the food of a time and a place. The time is prior to 1950, and the place is southern Mississippi.

Of course, since this is the food my momma made, it is also my definition of "comfort food." I love that phrase. What a warm and fuzzy, slightly chubby picture it conjures up. What does it mean, exactly? In my mind, comfort food is soft, boneless and almost inhalable. Like mashed potatoes and gravy, scalloped potatoes, the tenderest of meats, cornbread dressing, gravies, cheesy casseroles, macaroni and cheese, and banana pudding from a very large bowl (preferably after the rest of the family is asleep). Something that can be eaten faster than you can breathe through your nose. And to be comfort food, it must be eaten in such large quantities that a meal must be followed immediately by a nap.

There are a lot of things about old-fashioned Southern Mississippi food that just can't be done anymore. For one thing, we can never eat the quantity of food that my grandfather did when my momma first started cooking for him and the rest of the family. But God forbid anybody should ever have to work as hard as my uncles and granddad did. Imagine plowing all day behind a mule, digging wells by hand, or doing all that pulling, lifting, pushing, digging, hauling and sawing logs without power tools. All this in the dirt, the mud and the heat of a Mississippi summer or a freezing cold winter. And to hear the stories now, it seems like most of this energy was spent on ensuring that there was enough food to put on the table.

My yen to work as a storekeeper and to produce large amounts of food might have been inherited from Granddad. He opened the first general store in Lumberton, Mississippi, then bought the only hotel in town when he married Grandmother. Two boys later, he tore down the hotel, hauled the lumber two miles out of town and built a 16-room farmhouse. He dug a well, built a smokehouse and became a farmer. When Grandma went to work in 1933 as a welfare agent and Mother began to cook for the family, there were three sons and four daughters. Breakfast, dinner and supper for a family of nine required a whole lotta food. Brunswick stew was popular because rabbits and squirrels were plentiful and cheap. It took a lot of chickens to lay enough eggs and still have chickens enough left to fry for growing kids on Sunday.

Yeah, I said breakfast, dinner and supper. "Lunch" is another one of those modern innovations that's changed Southern cooking. Dinner was the main meal in the old days and it was taken in the middle of the day. Most folks ate dinner at home. When the Industrial Revolution took the work force away from the farms and into the factories, they came up with lunch. (Somebody important said that lunch is the amount of food you can hold in one hand.) Lunch boxes and happy hour probably debuted at about the same time.

Dinner has remained the main meal of the day in this country, but it has moved to the evening, in the time period that used to be known as suppertime. Supper was a light meal back then. (Sunday dinner is the exception to these changes in eating patterns. In the deep South, it still comes right after church lets out.)

In our retro-1950s Southern spirit at Threadgill's, we still call our meals breakfast, dinner and supper, although we only serve breakfast on the weekends these days. There don't seem to be many folks left who start every day with a big plate of eggs, grits and biscuits smothered with gravy. Now that the big meal of the day is eaten late in the day, it is no wonder that breakfast has lost some of its appeal. I guess breakfast has become the easiest meal of

◆

It's strange that although vegetables have always been at the center of Southern cooking, nobody thinks it's possible for Southern cooking to be good for you.

◆

the day to consume in a manner that conforms to the Food Pyramid and people don't want to go out to a restaurant for a bowl of cereal. I've included my favorite breakfast recipes in this book for those of you who have a hard day's work to do or who like to eat a big breakfast for lunch on the weekends like I do.

The dinner and supper recipes in this book fit into the classic Southern restaurant format known as "meat and three." A square meal needs four corners and that means a meat and three vegetables. Of course, our definitions of meat and vegetables are a little bizarre.

John Egerton, referred to as the poet laureate of Southern food by restaurant critic Mimi Sheraton, tells the story of taking a non-Southerner to a little meat and three restaurant in Tennessee. His guest was bewildered to discover that in this part of the world, catfish is categorized as a meat, and macaroni and cheese is among the vegetables. You'll also find gumbo, watermelon slices and pickles in the vegetable category, and shrimp, chicken livers and fried oysters in with the meats. I'd hate to have to start calling it the "flesh protein and three starch, vegetable or side dish" format, so just try and keep an open mind on meat and three.

And speaking of vegetables, if you're worried that all this Southern cooking is going to mean a lot of unhealthy meals, you're in for a surprise. If you had to pick the one thing that Threadgill's Southern cooking does best, it would have to be our vegetables. Lots of people come to Threadgill's and eat nothing else. If the recipes in this book do nothing else but make you fall in love with vegetables, I'll be a happy man.

It's strange that although vegetables have always been at the center of Southern cooking, nobody thinks that it's possible for Southern cooking to be good for you. Southern-style cooking has been under attack for many years now for being heavy, fatty and artery-clogging. John Egerton blames this unfair criticism on the self-appointed health-food experts.

"The food police have turned lard into the moral equivalent of crack cocaine," says Egerton. In truth, lard is a healthier fat than butter in terms of cholesterol content. But you can't convince anybody of that fact anymore, so we don't even try. We use vegetable oil like everybody else. Ain't it strange though, that the same people who would never dream of using lard to make a fluffy pie crust don't think twice about devouring high-fat meals at a burger chain several times a week. Go figure.

Food fads based on fear have caused other radical changes in the eating habits of Southerners. I have a display case in the Upstairs Store from the 1930s with decals on each end, one a Baby Ruth ad, the other for Butterfingers. The advertising slogan boldly printed in large type across each proclaims "RICH IN DEXTROSE!" My, how times have changed. In the 1970s, every good mother tried to protect her baby from the poisons in our diet. White sugar got slammed hard.

This is when the Southern habit of serving "sweet tea" began to disappear. At the same time soft drinks, which are loaded with sugars, saw sales soar. One 12-ounce Classic Coke contains the equivalent of 10 teaspoons of sugar.

Salt was blamed for hypertension and everyone got hyper about ridding their diet of it. Restaurants had to respond by undersalting their food, and a whole new industry of low-salt and salt-substitute products was created at a cost of billions of dollars. Later studies concluded that much of the concern was unwarranted, but the newspapers didn't carry that story. I guess "Salt Is Poison" makes a better headline than "Salt Isn't So Bad After All." Thank goodness Mellorine never caught on as a substitute for ice cream.

◆

It would give me a warm feeling to think that I might've helped somebody somewhere enjoy an old-fashioned Southern dinner like my momma used to make.

◆

When Egerton spoke to a group of Southern food lovers recently at Threadgill's, we served up a buffet of old-fashioned Southern cooking. At least, we thought of it as old-fashioned Southern cooking. But a guest in her sixties took us aside after the meal and set us straight. First of all, she made it very clear that the broccoli we used as an illustration on the invitation was never eaten in this area in the old days. She also pointed out that our green beans were underdone. "Green beans should melt on the tongue," she insisted. The tea we served should have been sweetened, she pointed out, and the pepper sauce should have been spiced with the tiny native chili pequins, not Louisiana peppers.

Her comments spoke volumes about the difference between the food we serve at Threadgill's, which is as close an approximation of Southern cooking as the public will accept, and authentic Southern cooking of the 1940s and '50s. Green beans that melt on your tongue may have once seemed wonderful, but nowadays our customers would send them back

as too mushy. And we have to leave the tea sweetening to the individual these days. As for the chili pequins, they are great, but as I explained to my charming critic, nobody bottles a commercial chili pequin hot sauce, since these peppers only grow wild. The next day she stopped by with a bottle of homemade hot sauce for me to try. It's sitting on my kitchen table and we are making plans to grow enough peppers next year to supply the tables at the restaurant.

There are other things we do at Threadgill's that Momma never would have done. We use aged beef of the highest quality to make our meatloaf. To her, meatloaf was an inexpensive way to get us full. She also would have been amazed to see us selling hundreds of chicken-fried chicken breasts each week. Chicken-fried chicken breast is something we made up because we can't get people to sit still long enough for us to make real fried chicken. We've also got some entrées like bronzed fish and chicken that Momma wouldn't recognize.

Many of our customers are couples, one a vegetarian and the other here for liver. Others are divided between the desire for old-fashioned comfort food and something light and healthy. We try to keep lots of folks happy. And what we've evolved in the process is a version of old-fashioned Southern cooking that makes as few compromises as possible but still fits into the lifestyles of our customers. I hope that the recipes in this book fit into your lifestyle too.

They aren't fancy recipes. Some of them are quick and easy dishes that will help you out on those frenzied weekday nights when dinner has to be quick. Some of them take a little longer. And when you decide to combine four recipes or more to make a classic meat and three dinner with cornbread and dessert, there's no denying you're going to be in for a little work.

But every once in a while, I hope this cookbook will inspire you to roll up your sleeves and go for it. It would give me a warm feeling to think that I might've helped somebody somewhere enjoy an old-fashioned Southern dinner like my momma used to make.

COOKING METHODS

The Threadgill's menu is a little unusual in that we offer the same foods prepared in several ways. Before you get confused trying to figure out the differences in the recipes, let's define our terms.

GRILLED: In our kitchen, this means charbroiled over high heat. Charbroiling first swept the backyards of the country in the '50s when husbands reentered the food chain during newfound leisure time. Flame-kissed became a byword for flavor as they singed burgers and steaks by the million. Lots of Texans insist that a steak must be cooked this way and we happily oblige.

COUNTRY STYLE: I personally prefer to pan-fry my steaks. Then while the table is being set I make a gravy or sopping sauce of some sort with the juices and the butter left in the pan. I call this pan-fried-with-gravy-method "country style."

CHICKEN-FRIED: In our version of this wonderful Southern tradition, meats are dipped in egg wash, dusted in seasoned flour, dipped in egg wash again and dropped into a deep fryer. The egg wash seals quickly and the juices of the meat are deliciously trapped by the crisp, golden crust.

BRONZED: This is a not-so-traditional but unusually tasty method of cooking that was introduced to Threadgill's by one of our early chefs, Glenn Bob Adams of New Orleans. The entrées are dipped in Cajun spices, then cooked on a flat grill with a little butter. Catfish, chicken breasts, steaks and pork chops are all wonderful when bronzed.

SOUTHWESTERN: These dishes are grill-smoked (preferably over charcoal or hardwood) and served with Smoked Corn Relish and Chipotle Cream Sauce. There is nothing about

this method that is remotely part of my history of Southern cooking. It is a way of tipping the hat to an innovative genius, Mark Miller, and his influence in creating a cuisine where once there was none. It is also delicious and easy.
SMOKING: Use your telephone to shop your local grocery stores and delis for smoked meats, or make smoking a special learning project. Its pleasurable return on invested time outweighs fishing, and it's safer to drink beer sitting in a chair in the yard next to a smoker than it is to drink beer in a boat. Don't limit yourself to typical barbecue fare. Stem tomatoes and smoke them for wonderful additions to salads. Smoke peppers of any sort. Invent your own smoked corn relish. Smoke several things at a time and put them up in freezer bags and jars.

EQUIPMENT

Obviously, you need a deep-fat fryer or a big high-sided frying pan to chicken-fry a steak, and you need a grill of some sort to make grilled or Southwestern dishes. Fried chicken requires a cast-iron skillet. Beyond that, the subject of kitchen equipment gets pretty personal. I haven't included any microwave instructions here because in my opinion, the only thing a microwave is good for is melting butter. And since I live in Texas and don't have to plug in my windowsill, I don't need a microwave to melt butter. (Oh, okay, they are great for reheating leftovers, but nobody writes much about leftovers in a restaurant cookbook.)

In the Threadgill's cookbook library there's a corner bookshelf full of old books and pamphlets too brittle to handle but on rare occasion. Two of my favorites were both published in 1914. One is a beautifully illustrated kitchen equipment catalogue titled *The John Van Range Company, Implements for Culinary Purposes*. The other is called *Household Discoveries and Mrs. Curtis's Cook Book*. The two of them illustrate the fact that most of the necessary equipment for preparing good food was already invented long before you could buy an aerosol spray to grease your Teflon muffin tin before pouring in your instant muffin mix. Most of the basic recipes of today are printed therein as well. These publications also illustrate that if you keep an eye open, there are great treasures available to collectors for the tiniest sums.

Perhaps this is an appropriate place to insert a word about collecting. First, you need to know what is available new and what it costs. There are decent cast-iron pots and pans available at reasonable prices, sometimes a third the cost of an identical item at a tourist-trap antique shop. Other times you'll happen upon cast-iron items that are no longer manufactured or perhaps just available in much lighter versions, in which case it might make sense to buy them used. Browse your local restaurant supply dealers and ask to look at catalogues. Second, if an item might lead to a meal, buy it. Fishing lures, cookbooks with one tempting recipe, an old breakfast skillet with partitions for eggs and bacon that you're attracted to—what the heck. Third, if it is attractive and if you have a place to display it, grab it. If you are going to put it in a drawer, pass it up.

The microwave is the last in a long line of what we used to call "labor-saving devices." Kitchen utensils, appliances, tools and gadgets designed to save Momma time and energy in preparing the traditional nightly feast. The modern evolution of the kitchen had its glorious beginnings in the development of the household ice box and the gas stove.

The drawers beside my momma's stove contained a history of her kitchen. In one drawer there were warranty cards and instructions that came with every kitchen appliance she ever owned: the mixer, the electric skillet, the pressure cooker, several toasters and toaster ovens, a waffle iron, even instructions on how to efficiently use the chest freezer to feed the family better for less. There was no evidence of a wok, a microwave or a salad spinner. Meanwhile, her beautiful O'Keefe and Merrit stove had a griddle in the middle and an adjustable broiler for our steaks, like all high-quality residential stoves of the day. I've often wondered why modern stoves aren't made with griddles anymore. In some ways it seems like we're moving backwards in the kitchen equipment department.

Appliances designed to keep your kitchen neat and tidy are often responsible for food without soul. Love is messy and so is good cooking.

But God forbid we should go back to the days of my grandma's kitchen. Tradition is great, but I seldom hear anybody lamenting the bygone days of hauling ice, chopping wood and making your own soap. Some modern kitchen gadgets may be useless but some are indispensable, and the rest fall into the gray area in between. The key is to choose appliances that help you cook better and that you are really going to use. Forget about the ones that are designed to cook your food without messing up the kitchen.

The major benefit of the bread machine is that it bakes bread without making a mess. Your kitchen will stay clean, but every loaf of bread you bake will be shaped like a coffee can. Unfortunately, a lot of people choose appliances based on this criterion. And they avoid some great inventions such as smokers, grills and stovetop griddles because they make a mess. Some people would rather go hungry than have to clean up. It's no wonder Teflon made such a big hit.

The recipes in this book can be executed with the simplest of kitchen utensils, provided you don't mind taking your time and making a mess. Chicken-frying in a big frying pan is guaranteed to get a thin skin of grease all over the place. A food processor will not only speed things up, it will also keep stuff from falling on the floor while you're chopping.

But don't let any of these modern conveniences change the way you cook. In my opinion, appliances designed to keep your kitchen neat and tidy are often responsible for food without soul. Love is messy and so is good cooking.

Ingredients

My mother occasionally reverted to the hunter-gatherer era when she came across free food. When it came to food, her labor was never figured in as an expense. Whether chasing crabs on the Texas coast, shelling peas, or gathering figs or pecans by the bushel to crack and shell, she was the family's indentured food servant.

Her attitudes were shaped by the Great Depression. The rich folks in Lumberton, Mississippi, were the Bass family. They claimed to have the largest pecan orchard in the world. When Beulah and Woody chose to build a home in Austin, they decided against the $40-per-acre land on the hillsides with glorious views of the Hill Country. That's where all the rich folks in Austin live today. But my folks didn't see the sun setting over the lake; what they saw was rocky soil. If the Depression were to return, the ground would never do for raising enough food to feed a family.

Instead, they bought a tumbling down old house on a double lot west of town, with enough good dirt to allow for a large garden if it was needed. I think what really closed the deal were the magnificent pecan trees that graced the property. They made us a tiny bit like the Bass family.

Years later, when a bumper crop of their pecans coincided with the worst pecan crop in history back in Mississippi, Beulah and Woody spent the month before Christmas cracking and shelling in the living room each night after work while they watched television. For Christmas presents that year they shipped more than 400 pounds of pecans back to their family and friends in Mississippi. Momma loved those pecan trees almost as much as she loved her garden.

I love Sandra's garden. But few endeavors can be as satisfying or as disappointing as tending a garden. I had a moment of gardening truth last summer. After harvesting a bumper crop of tomatoes, I spent all day cooking a tomato sauce recipe that I like. I was able to use all fresh ingredients from our garden. It was great.

But as I was pouring the sauce into jars, it dawned on me how much it looked like the brand of tomato sauce I often buy at the grocery store. And how much it tasted like it too. It was a little disappointing. After all, this isn't the Depression anymore and there's no shortage of good things to eat. The bad news is that spending my time and energy making tomato sauce isn't always worth it anymore. The good news is that when I run out of my homemade sauce, my grocer will have the same thing waiting for me 365 days a year. Or maybe even something better.

◆

Tradition is great, but I seldom hear anybody lamenting the bygone days of hauling ice, chopping wood and making your own soap.

◆

The grocery business has changed drastically in the last few years. At least it has in my neighborhood. I shop at a store called H-E-B Central Market. Some people in central Texas drive over 100 miles each way to visit Austin each week just to buy their groceries at Central Market. The place stocks 16,000 square feet of perfect produce, displays 75 running feet of fresh seafood and offers 500 kinds of cheese besides the huge prepared foods section. It's a new concept in food stores that has been widely praised as the leading edge in the American grocery business.

Grocers across the country are building similar stores. They are trying to compete with the restaurants in your city. You can help them help you by telling them what you want. Get to know your butcher. You'd be surprised how many tricks he knows that he never has a chance to show anybody. He'd just love to cut you something special. Get to know your store manager. He wants your business. If you are dealing with a leading grocery chain, the store manager has a very good job. Finding ingredients for you is an important part of it. Ask his advice. If he doesn't have what you want, ask him to order it.

And while you're at the grocery store, take another look at some of those tomato sauces, salsas, canned and frozen vegetables and all the other convenience foods that you never buy.

Homegrown Tomatoes

by Guy Clark

Ain't nothin in the world that I like better
than bacon and lettuce and homegrown tomatoes
Up in the mornin' out in the garden
get you a ripe 'un don't get a hard one
Plant 'em in the spring eat 'em in the summer
All winter without 'em's a culinary bummer
I forget all about the sweatin and diggin
evertime I go out and pick me a big one

CHORUS
Homegrown tomatoes homegrown tomatoes
Wha'd life be without homegrown tomatoes
Only two things money can't buy
That's true love and homegrown tomatoes

I've been out to eat and that's for sure
But it's nothin' a homegrown tomato won't cure
Put 'em in a salad put 'em in a stew
You can make your very own tomato juice
Eat 'em with eggs eat 'em with gravy
Eat 'em with beans pinto or navy
Put 'em on the side put 'em in the middle
Put a homegrown tomato on a hotcake griddle

If I's to change this life that I lead
I'd be Johnny Tomato seed
'Cause I know that this country needs
Homegrown tomatoes in every yard you see
When I die don't bury me
in a box in a cemetery
Out in the garden would be much better
I could be pushing up homegrown tomatoes

Personally, I think it's time for a change of heart about convenience foods. We have gotten so agitated about overly processed and bad convenience foods that we sometimes turn up our noses at good stuff. And in the process we are throwing out the baby with the bathwater. Eating bad food is a bad idea. Convenient and easy are not bad ideas. Satisfaction and nourishment are goals that can be pursued laboriously or with cunning and stealth.

Take black-eyed peas, for instance. Fresh black-eyed peas are wonderful, but the season doesn't last long, so they aren't available very often. Dried black-eyed peas take hours to make and can taste mealy. But canned black-eyed peas taste great all year round. Every pea is perfect. There's not a teaspoon of trash in the whole can. So why not buy them?

Don't get me wrong. I think the reaction against processed foods has brought about some great innovations. I guess the idea behind buying foods in bulk was to buy the stuff and not the can or the jar it came in. But the side effect was to give you a chance to buy just what you need for tonight's recipe. What a great idea.

The truth is that I've become a little more open-minded about convenience foods since we started freezing Threadgill's vegetables and selling them in grocery stores. This project opened my mind to a lot of new ideas. And when I read that the Amerindians of New England were freezing large quantities of succotash in the snow banks so they could chip off enough for dinner on a winter's night in the 1600s, I also realized that a lot of convenience foods weren't new ideas at all.

There's no question that fresh tomatoes from your garden and perfect fresh vegetables from the farmers' market or the grocery store are superior in every way to canned or frozen stuff. But if I have one tip about fresh foods, it's this: Use them right away!

Fresh vegetables are great for a little while. But when they're all wilted up in the bottom of the crisper drawer they are simply a waste of money. By all means, buy fresh vegetables, fresh fish and fresh chicken when you can get them. But then use them fast. If you find that you're buying fresh stuff and then letting it get old or throwing it in the freezer, then you are really wasting your money.

I also dare you to try this experiment: Buy some fresh spinach. Clean it carefully to remove the grit. Stem it, chop it up and cook it down into spinach casserole or creamed spinach. Now do the same thing starting with frozen spinach. Compare the results. Can you taste any difference?

Now tell me, which cost more, the convenience food or the fresh one? Which one took more time to prepare? Which one keeps better if you can't use it right away? Of course there are lots of salads and wilted spinach recipes that require fresh spinach. But if you're making spinach casserole, what's the big difference?

Take your grocer's advice about interesting and convenient new products. Keep an open mind about ingredients and make your own decisions by experimenting with foods in your own kitchen. And stop apologizing if the ingredients you decide you like are also convenient.

ATTITUDE

Time and temperature get a lot of ink in modern cookbooks. But once you've turned the knobs that set the timer and the heat level, don't forget the spirit of the thing. No method, technique or ingredient will serve you better in the kitchen than that wonderful state of mind that I think of as the **Good Food Attitude**. The attitude is part and parcel of great Southern cooking. The glee of sharpening knives, the desire to go shopping and the urge to garden or forage—all of these are symptoms of an attitude coming on.

And with the attitude comes great eating. You know you've locked on it when you find yourself sautéing onion, celery and garlic instead of turning on the television, when you begin to anticipate the arrival of the spring seed catalogues, when the seasons find their meaning in the produce department of your neighborhood store.

You know you're in touch with your food when there are certain things you feel you must do at certain times of year, like roast some ears of fresh sweet corn, search out the perfect watermelon, bake some autumn apples, spot the perfect asparagus, cook a pot of beets.

Prowling around farmers' markets and roadside stands will keep you in touch with the seasons of your own local specialties. It is not the bargains that these places offer on fresh produce that's important, it is the opportunity to get something wonderful while it's in peak season that's exciting.

Once you've got the attitude, don't let little annoyances throw you off. So what if your teenage daughter is on a diet and will only eat Special K for dinner? Why should your enjoyment of food have to suffer? Too bad if your husband doesn't like vegetables. Tell him, "These aren't vegetables, these are very special casseroles." Don't let anybody else's lack of the Good Food Attitude ruin yours.

And don't be discouraged if all your cooking masterpieces don't turn out perfect....

"Boss, the lady in the green dress over there in the first booth says that the peach cobbler tastes like onions."

It happens to the best of us.

POTATOES
Campbell's
THREADGILL'S
Mexican

CHAPTER THREE

THE PANTRY

TWO THINGS I MISS from the "old place" in Mississippi are the mud porch and the pantry. The mud porch was between the kitchen and the backyard. It separated the house from the mud and muck that otherwise would have been tracked in from the fields, the smokehouse and the soap kettle. It was where coats and boots came off and were left till after a meal and where the first washing machine was put. The mud finally got civilized and mud porches gave way to garages connected to houses by breezeways. That's where we shelled peas and churned ice cream and wished for breezes. Air conditioning and television zapped the breezeway, and turned it into a den. I never made the adjustment from screen wire, gliders and hammocks to jalousie windows and Naugahyde recliners. I just liked being closer to the lightning bugs.

Mother always had a loaded pantry. When she was growing up in the country, she and Aunt Bub and Granddad would can up 500 jars a season of vegetables to be eaten in the next few months. When she moved to the city and started the nursery school she industrialized her pantry efforts. The walk-in food closet was efficient but it was also an effort to comfort us by showing that we were prepared against the possible return of the Depression. The pantry became a psychological food bank into which deposits were made when grocery stores put on good sales. It was into this food library I would be sent to fetch items Mother needed as she prepared a meal. I'd usually stand and stare at shelves loaded with "staples" and could almost never find what I was sent to get. I must have heard a hundred times, "If it was a snake it would bite you." After a few minutes of gawking I'd forget what I was looking for, lost in amazement at all the things Mother had in there and at how she really expected me to find anything. Truth be known, I probably learned to read in the pantry, looking for things like Calumet and Arm & Hammer while wishing they were Hydrox and Oreos. (The old grocery store signs used to read

"Groceries: Fancy and Staple." We had mostly Staple.)

In 1952, soon after we got our first car with an automatic transmission, the folks bought a big chest freezer. The pantry burst with new treasures, purchased on sale and hauled home to our food bank from whatever grocers and butchers and bakers had advertised a really good discount. You'd have thought we were Eskimos and Momma was stocking the larder for a six-month blizzard. We were not going hungry, no matter what. The principle was simple: Plan ahead. The execution required a bit of shopping.

Today the pantry has turned into kitchen cabinets and big, modern refrigerators. I present the Pantry chapter first to help you think of ways to make easier the tasks of large meals and special occasions. Most of these items I've given you recipes for are available at your better neighborhood grocers. Others, such as Jezebel Sauce, Jalapeño Honey Mustard, Chipotle Cream Sauce, Homemade Mayonnaise, and Blue Cheese Dressing can be made ahead of time to have on hand, like a magic wand. Chicken Stock and Spinach Casserole should be treated the same way. Make a bigger batch than you intend to use and freeze the rest in quarts. Whammo! They are better than gold bullion in your food bank and you'll feel richer than Scrooge McDuck.

◆

Look for an old butcher. He knows more than you want to know and yet hardly anybody ever asks him anything very smart.

◆

STOCKS

If I had to point out one single image that best represents the Threadgill's menu, it would be the row of stock pots left to burble and bubble and simmer all night, every night, in the commissary. Those and big pans of roasting bones would be nearly perfect icons of scratch cooking. Both are necessary for the perfect Southern plate. Without them there would be no perfect gravy. And certainly not the hundreds of gallons we make each day. Skillet gravy, made after frying chicken or chicken-fried steak, is wonderful. But if I'm going to tell you all the secrets of our menu, I've got to run you through this procedure, too.

Freeze your scraps whenever you cook roasts or chickens. Or use them right away to make stock and freeze the stock. Roasting bones bought from your butcher are a good value and a very good way to begin a relationship with a butcher. He doesn't sell bones to very many of his customers. Right away he will know that you have an attitude about food and he'll take more interest in you than if you were buying five pounds of hamburger meat. Ask him to tell you the weight of various pieces of meat in his display case. "How much does that boned pork loin weigh?" (It will usually weigh between 1 and 2½ pounds.) "Is it much trouble to cut one that's 4 pounds?" ("No, not at all!" should be the quick and pleasant answer.) A budding relationship with a butcher is born. Look for an old butcher. He knows more than you want to know and yet hardly anybody ever asks him anything very smart. If you can make it apparent that you want something extra good instead of seeming to want something extra cheap, you can make a good, friendly consultant in a hurry.

CHICKEN STOCK is the easiest, i.e. quickest, stock to make, and because we don't have any totally committed vegans around my house, it is as versatile as we need. When you finish you have chicken soup, and with next to no additional effort you have tortilla soup.

VEGETABLE STOCK is just as easy; it just needs to cook a bit longer to achieve full flavor because you don't begin with as much flavor in the pot.

BEEF STOCK is a real departure from today's trend of cooking as little as possible. The process will charge the atmosphere in an underused residential kitchen. The satisfaction quotient is high.

At home it is easier to boil beef bones and omit roasting them. You'll still get good stock. It just won't be as nearly perfect without the extra trouble. Harry Aiken, founder of Austin's Night Hawk Restaurants (who led the racial integration of Austin's eateries), had a wonderful slogan: "There is no accident about quality." This is especially true of the brown beef stock. The rendered marrow of the bones, scraped from the bottom of the pan, is the essence of deep, dark brown flavor.

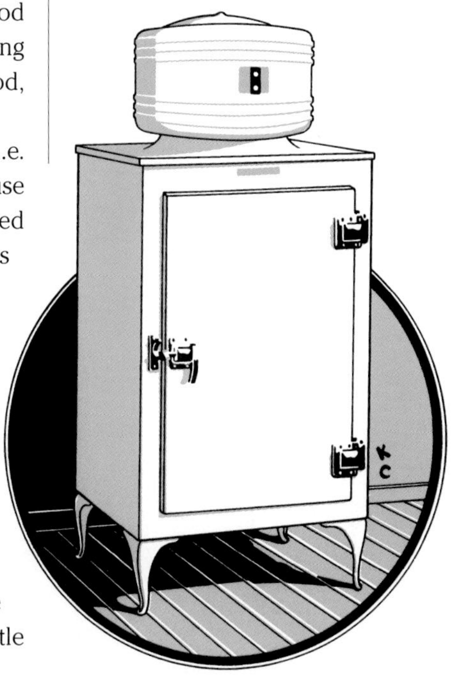

BEEF STOCK

5 pounds cut beef bones, in 3- or 4-inch chunks
1 large onion, chopped into 1-inch pieces
1 stalk celery, chopped into 1-inch pieces
2 large carrots, chopped into 1-inch pieces
5 cloves garlic, split
Roast beef scraps, if available
2 teaspoons peppercorns
5 or 6 sprigs parsley
2 bay leaves
2½ gallons cold water

ROAST BONES at 400° for about 2 hours. Add cut vegetables for the last 15 minutes. Scrape out the marrow and reserve. Put all ingredients into stock pot and bring to a boil. Reduce heat and gently simmer, occasionally skimming fat from the top, for 8 hours. Strain the stock and remove fat from top. Stock may be further reduced for more concentrated flavor by boiling longer. **Makes 1½ gallons.**

CHICKEN STOCK

4 pounds chicken bones or pieces
2 large carrots, cut into 1-inch pieces
1 bunch celery, cut into 1-inch pieces
1 large onion, cut into 1-inch pieces
3 cloves garlic, split
2 bay leaves
5 to 6 sprigs parsley
1 teaspoon thyme
2 teaspoons peppercorns
2½ gallons cold water

ROAST BONES for 30 minutes in 350° oven. Put everything into a stock pot and bring to a full boil. Reduce heat and simmer for at least 2 hours. Strain the stock and remove the fat from top before using. **Makes 6 quarts.**

☛ I'd rather have a large stove than a limousine. You can't make stocks and gravy in a limousine. Besides, I drive a pickup truck. I'm always finding an old stove that I need to carry home.

TURKEY STOCK

4 pounds turkey bones or pieces
2 large carrots, cut into 1-inch pieces
1 bunch celery, cut into 1-inch pieces
1 large onion, cut into 1-inch pieces
3 cloves garlic, split
2 bay leaves
5 to 6 sprigs parsley
1 teaspoon sage
1 teaspoon thyme
2 teaspoons peppercorns
2½ gallons cold water

ROAST BONES for 30 minutes in 350° oven. Put everything into a stock pot and bring to a full boil. Reduce heat and simmer for at least 2 hours. Strain the stock and remove the fat from top before using. **Makes 6 quarts.**

STOCK FROM ROAST TURKEY: Roast turkey neck for 30 minutes. Use neck and half the listed ingredients to make half a recipe of turkey stock. You will have enough stock to make pan gravy from the roast turkey drippings.

☛ This is an easy one to take advantage of during the holiday turkey craze.

VEGETABLE STOCK

1 bunch celery, chopped into 1-inch pieces
2 large carrots, chopped into 1-inch pieces
1 large onion, chopped into 1-inch pieces
4 cloves garlic, split
1 large Idaho potato, chopped into 1-inch pieces (optional)
2 teaspoons peppercorns
5 to 6 sprigs parsley
2 bay leaves
2 gallons cold water

BRING INGREDIENTS to a boil and reduce to a simmer. Leave to simmer about 2 hours and strain and use. **Makes 6 quarts.**

☛ We make this vegetable stock because we have so many vegetarian friends.

SOUTHERN SPICES

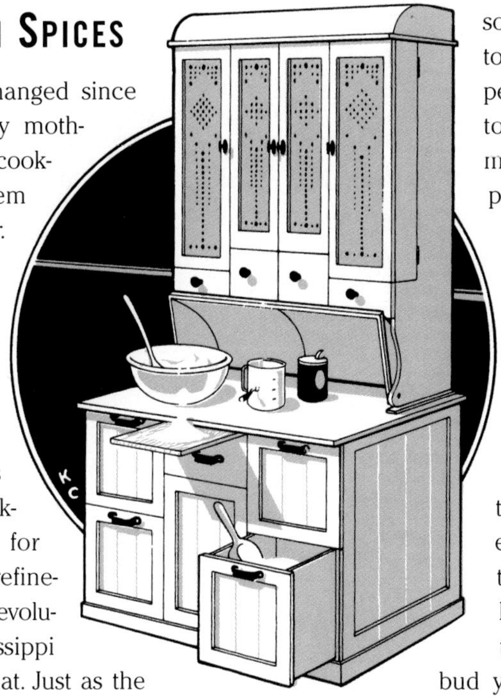

Things have changed since the days of my mother's Southern cooking, some of them for the better. Seasonings are one example. Momma used garlic some, but nowhere near the quantity we use nowadays in Southern cooking. This taste for seasonings is a refinement, a sign of evolution in the Mississippi farm food format. Just as the perceived need for shined boots became more important when we started walking on pavement more often than behind a mule, the taste for seasonings is a part of a more cosmopolitan way of life in the Old South.

The seasonings that we make at the restaurant are a necessity in a high-volume place like Threadgill's. High-quality seasonings similar to what we use are available to you in first-class grocery stores, but we save a ton by making them ourselves and end up with seasonings that are personalized, unique to Threadgill's. My personal tastes run to hotter, spicier, more tart flavor profiles than the average customer and therefore what I do at home is not what I do at the restaurant. As the taste buds get older they need sharper flavors to wake them up. I knew I was getting up there in taste-bud years when, one morning not long after my 50th birthday, I suddenly craved a glass of buttermilk for the first time in my life. I let the craving grow, slowly, gradually, for a couple of years until this year. Sure enough, when I tried it I loved it, and now it is part of my daily diet. It is hard to believe that it is so low in fat when it satisfies in a way so similar to blue cheese dressing. Anyhow, the blends that follow are for the reasonable palates of my customers. My personal ones almost all contain more peppers, vinegar, lemon, etc.

The taste for seasonings is a part of a more cosmopolitan way of life in the Old South.

Meat Seasoning

$^1/_2$ cup flaked salt
4 tablespoons black pepper
2 tablespoons white pepper
$1^1/_2$ teaspoons cayenne pepper
2 tablespoons granulated onion
$1^1/_2$ teaspoons ground cumin
4 tablespoons dry granulated garlic
2 tablespoons paprika

Mix ingredients well. Store in a glass jar or plastic container. Keep tightly sealed. Shake before each use to prevent settling.

Poultry Seasoning

$^1/_2$ cup flaked salt
4 tablespoons black pepper
2 tablespoons white pepper
$1^1/_2$ teaspoons cayenne pepper
2 tablespoons granulated onion
$1^1/_2$ teaspoons ground cumin
$1^1/_2$ teaspoons sage
4 tablespoons dry granulated garlic
2 tablespoons paprika
$1^1/_2$ teaspoons thyme

Mix ingredients well. Store in a glass jar or plastic container. Keep tightly sealed. Shake before each use to prevent settling.

Vegetable Seasoning

1 cup salt
2 tablespoons black pepper
6 tablespoons white pepper
4 tablespoons cayenne pepper
2 tablespoons granulated onion
4 tablespoons dry granulated garlic
2 tablespoons dry mustard

Mix ingredients well. Store in a glass jar or plastic container. Keep tightly sealed. Shake before each use to prevent settling.

Seafood Seasoning

½ cup flaked salt
2 tablespoons black pepper
2 tablespoons cayenne pepper
3 tablespoons granulated onion
3 tablespoons dry granulated garlic
2 tablespoons leaf oregano
2 tablespoons thyme
½ cup paprika
2 tablespoons basil

Mix ingredients well. Store in a glass jar or plastic container. Keep tightly sealed. Shake before each use to prevent settling.

BBQ Rub

1 pound paprika
4 ounces black pepper
4 ounces cayenne pepper
4 ounces dry granulated garlic

MIX INGREDIENTS WELL. Store in a glass jar or plastic container. Keep tightly sealed. Shake before each use to prevent settling.

Sauces, Dressings and Such

When my father-in-law became a heart patient, the doctor told him to eat a lot of salads. So he developed his own recipe. He topped a wedge of iceberg with chopped eggs, bacon and mayonnaise.

If you are eating salad in order to lose weight or cut down on the fat in your diet, you have to decide how many bad things you really need to make your salad palatable.

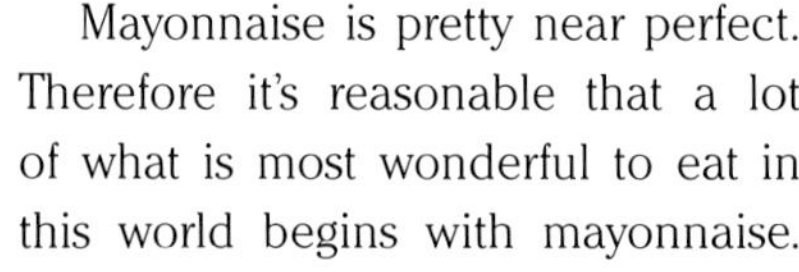

Mayonnaise is pretty near perfect. Therefore it's reasonable that a lot of what is most wonderful to eat in this world begins with mayonnaise. Old, encyclopedic cookbooks sometimes have dozens of salad dressing recipes that begin with a cup of mayonnaise. The effort to make your own homemade batch of mayonnaise will make you feel wonderful and give you the excuse to consume hundreds of extra calories, high in fat and cholesterol, that obviously are meant to be consumed or they wouldn't taste so good.

MAYONNAISE

1 egg
1 teaspoon salt
$^1/_4$ teaspoon sugar
$^1/_4$ teaspoon dry mustard
Dash cayenne pepper
Dash black pepper
Dash paprika
1 tablespoon vinegar
$1^1/_2$ cups salad oil
1 tablespoon lemon juice

PLACE EGG, salt, sugar, mustard, cayenne pepper, black pepper, paprika, and vinegar in mixing bowl. Slowly add ½ cup salad oil, a tablespoon at a time, while beating at high speed. Gradually add remaining oil, then lemon juice, and continue to beat at high speed for about 3 minutes or until thick. Refrigerate. **Makes 2 cups.**

☛ For salads it is easy to begin with mayonnaise and invent variations.

LEMON (OR LIME) MAYONNAISE

1 cup mayonnaise
1 tablespoon bottled capers, chopped
$^1/_2$ teaspoon salt
1 teaspoon prepared mustard
$^1/_4$ cup lemon (or lime) juice

TO 1 CUP mayonnaise add other ingredients and refrigerate until ready to use.

☛ When I was living in Zihuatanejo, Mexico, in the mid '60s, I rented a room at Mamma Elvira's house for 40 dollars a month. It came with three meals a day and laundry. Meals were eaten on a porch not 50 yards from the beach, and at the end of the porch was a lime tree within reach of the corner table. For the six months I lived there, I squeezed fresh lime juice on almost everything I ate. I still consume more tart flavors than most people and if my life turns out to be half as long as it has been happy, I suspect that the added shelf life might be from this habit.

BLUE CHEESE DRESSING

1½ teaspoons apple cider vinegar
¾ teaspoon dry mustard
3 tablespoons parsley, finely chopped
1 tablespoon sugar
¾ teaspoon white pepper
3 cups mayonnaise
1 pound blue cheese, crumbled
¾ cup sour cream
1½ teaspoons Worcestershire sauce
⅓ cup buttermilk

MIX THE DRY INGREDIENTS with vinegar. Add other ingredients and blend well. Thin as needed with buttermilk, ¼ to ⅓ cup. **Makes 1½ quarts.**

☛ There is more reason to make this recipe at home than some others in this category, because blue cheese dressing of this quality is just about impossible to find in the grocery. Notice how some blue-cheese-in-a-jar brags about being creamy. Really it should apologize for being creamy. The chunks of blue cheese that are necessary to qualify the dressing as excellent simply melted when the jar was packed. To be "shelf stable," it was packed at a heat level that ensured certain death to bacteria. That heat melted the chunks of cheese. Also beware those jars that proudly proclaim "Chunky!" blue cheese dressing. If the jar is on an unrefrigerated shelf, the chunks are not really lumps of cheese at all but instead a soy product with a higher melting point, added to the recipe to give the "mouth-feel" so important in the food processing industry. The blue cheese at

Threadgill's has such large and tangy chunks of cheese that you might be tempted to slice them and make a sandwich.

HOT BACON DRESSING FOR SPINACH SALAD

1/4 cup onion, chopped
1/4 pound bacon, diced
3/4 cup water
1/2 cup cider vinegar
1/4 cup sugar
1 teaspoon salt
1/4 teaspoon pepper

FRY ONIONS and bacon together until onions are clear and bacon is crisp. Drain off fat and reserve. Combine ½ cup each water and vinegar. Heat to boiling. Add sugar, salt, and pepper. Blend remaining ¼ cup water and fat from bacon to a smooth paste. Stir into hot liquid. Return to boiling. Mixture will thicken slightly. Cook about 10 minutes. Add onion and bacon and serve at once. **Makes 2 cups.**

☛ Sweet and sour once again is the secret to putting a smile in a bite. From the sweet tip of the tongue to the tang toward the back by the jaw, this is it.

JALAPEÑO HONEY MUSTARD

1 quart mayonnaise
1 cup honey
4 ounces Creole mustard
1 cup jalapeño, minced

MIX THOROUGHLY and refrigerate. Always stir before using. **Makes 1½ quarts.**

☛ If you are going to fix just one of these dressings, choose Jalapeño Honey Mustard. It is the runaway hit of the decade in the restaurant. I mix it into coleslaw, use it as a dip, mix it with egg yolks for quick and spicy deviled eggs and spread it on sandwiches. Keep it away from the baby.

VINEGAR AND OIL

1 1/3 cups red wine vinegar
1/2 teaspoon dry mustard
1/2 teaspoon sugar
1 teaspoon black pepper
1/2 teaspoon white pepper
1/2 teaspoon salt
1 tablespoon parsley, minced
2 teaspoons garlic, minced
4 cups canola salad oil

MIX THE DRY INGREDIENTS with the vinegar. Add minced parsley and garlic and blend in the oil. Refrigerate. **Makes 1 1/2 quarts.**

THOUSAND ISLAND

1 hard-boiled egg, grated
1 tablespoon green bell pepper, minced
2 tablespoons onion, minced
1 tablespoon pimientos, diced
2 cups mayonnaise
1 tablespoon sweet relish
1/2 teaspoon Worcestershire sauce
1 cup chili sauce
1/2 teaspoon prepared horseradish
1/2 teaspoon dry mustard

COMBINE all ingredients slowly and blend on slow speed until well mixed, about 3 minutes. **Makes 1 quart.**

BBQ SAUCE

2 cloves garlic
1 orange, split
1 yellow onion, split
$1/2$ cup brown sugar
1 bay leaf
$1/2$ cup honey
16 ounces tomato sauce
14 ounces ketchup (1 regular size bottle)
$1/2$ cup A.1. Steak Sauce
$1/4$ cup prepared mustard
2 teaspoons Tabasco Sauce
2 ounces Worcestershire sauce
2 tablespoons red wine vinegar
4 ounces bock beer

COMBINE all ingredients and bring to a boil, stirring to keep them from burning, then reduce to a simmer, stirring occasionally. Simmer about 1 hour, then remove from heat and strain. Refrigerate unused portion. **Makes about 1 quart.**

☛ Rather than get into the endless discussion of which barbecue sauce is better than which, I'd suggest that the thing to do is accept the challenge and try to become an authority on what is available in your neighborhood and decide which you like best. I'll wager that several are really very good, and you can gather them all for a very pleasant sampling and for very little money. Think of it as your own private BBQ sauce festival. It might also be a good time to bring home several different beers and a sampling of different sausages—get some chicken or whatever you prefer to barbecue with which to sample whatever you find. Whip up a couple of recipes to add to the fun and decide what you really prefer. If you choose to be a bit more scholarly, pick up a copy of *The Ultimate Barbecue Sauce Cookbook* by Jim Auchmutey and Susan Puckett (Longstreet Press, 1995). This little book is about as complete as you'll ever need and begins with "Song to Barbecue Sauce" by my favorite poet, Roy Blount, Jr.

Just be sure, whatever you do, don't make the mistake of asking Rick Schmidt at Kreutz Market in Lockhart, Texas, "Where's the sauce?"

He's past the age where he'll rip off his cap to answer you, but you'll notice that the heat is not all coming from the pit in the floor. There's no need for a sauce if the meat is good. Oven-BBQed chicken, basted in a sweet, red, sticky sauce, hardly fits anyone's definition of BBQ, but if you happen upon it as a lunch special in an out-of-the-way shanty, you're likely to discover that finger-lickin' good doesn't limit itself to the Colonel's chicken.

Song to Barbecue Sauce

by Roy Blount, Jr.

Brush it on chicken, slosh it on pork,
Eat it with fingers, not with a fork.
I could eat barbecued turtle or squash—
I could eat tar paper cooked and awash
In barbecue sauce.

Nothing can gloss
Over barbecue sauce.

CREOLE SAUCE

4 tablespoons butter or margarine
½ cup yellow onion, diced
1 green bell pepper, sliced
½ cup celery, sliced
1 clove garlic, minced

2 pounds tomatoes, diced
1 cup Chicken Stock (see recipe, page 34)
2 green onions, chopped
4 cups tomato sauce
½ teaspoon cayenne pepper
1 bay leaf
1 teaspoon sugar
1 teaspoon gumbo filé
½ teaspoon Tabasco Sauce

MELT BUTTER in a large skillet and lightly sauté diced onions, bell pepper, and celery. Add garlic and green onions, then transfer to a heavy 3- or 4-quart pot. Add tomato sauce, diced tomatoes, and chicken stock. Bring to a boil while stirring constantly to avoid scorching. Add rest of ingredients and reduce heat to simmering, stirring often. Simmer 20 to 25 minutes or until flavors are well blended. **Makes 2 quarts.**

☛ Next to homegrown tomatoes themselves, this is about the best thing there is to eat that comes in red.

CHIPOTLE CREAM SAUCE

◆

12 ounces Mexican sour cream
3 ounces canned chipotle peppers in adobo sauce

WHIP IN BLENDER until smooth and pink. Refrigerate.

☛ This is almost too easy to be this good. Don't feel guilty, though; just because I don't have any secrets doesn't mean that you can't have a few. Don't tell them how easy it is. Just offer to make them some next time you're going to all the trouble anyway.

COCKTAIL SAUCE

$3^1/_2$ cups ketchup
2 teaspoons Worcestershire sauce
4 tablespoons horseradish
Juice of 2 lemons
$^1/_2$ teaspoon black pepper

COMBINE all ingredients and mix well. **Makes 1 quart.**

JEZEBEL SAUCE

1 12-ounce jar pineapple preserves
1 10-ounce jar apple jelly
2 teaspoons dry mustard
$^1/_4$ cup horseradish

COMBINE all ingredients and mix well. Refrigerate. **Makes 3 cups.**

☛ This is the most extreme example of sweet and hot, and it might prove that we are a bit Asian. It is perfect with pork, and if you've never tried it I guarantee you will find it worth the very little bit of effort it takes to whip up a batch.

PASTALAYA BASE

4 tablespoons margarine or butter
1 cup yellow onion, diced
$^1/_2$ cup celery, diced
$^1/_2$ cup green bell peppers, diced

2 tablespoons garlic, minced
3 large jalapeño peppers, seeded and minced
4 pounds tomatoes, diced
3 tablespoons Poultry Seasoning (see recipe, page 38)

PREHEAT OVEN to 400°. Sauté onion in half the margarine until caramelized. Remove from heat and set aside. Sauté celery and bell pepper in remaining margarine until very soft. Add garlic and jalapeño. Add diced tomato and cook over medium heat, stirring until reduced about one half. Add cooked onion and seasoning and bake in 400° oven, stirring every 15 minutes. Continue cooking until very thick and reduced to about 3 cups. This should take about an hour. **Makes 3 cups.**

CITRUS BUTTER

1 small orange
1 medium lemon
1 clove garlic
1/2 pound (2 sticks) butter, softened
1/4 teaspoon black pepper
Dash salt
1/2 teaspoon tarragon
1 teaspoon soy sauce

PEEL THE TOP LAYER (colored part only) of orange and lemon rind. Chop rind and garlic very fine. Squeeze juice from the fruit and set aside. Cream butter in mixer, adding garlic, rind, and spices. Add soy sauce and reserved juice. Whip until thoroughly blended. **Makes 1 1/2 cups.**

NOTE: Extra citrus butter may be frozen.

☛ There are not many things you can do to improve on the taste of an aged, Certified Angus steak, but this is one and it is too easy to pass up.

Tartar Sauce

$^1/_3$ cup capers
2 green onions
2 sprigs parsley
4 large green olives
1 quart mayonnaise
Juice of $^1/_2$ lemon
1 tablespoon sweet relish
1 teaspoon Tabasco Sauce

FINELY CHOP capers, green onions, parsley, and olives. Blend all ingredients well. Refrigerate. **Makes 1 quart.**

Horseradish Sour Cream Sauce

1 cup sour cream
$^1/_2$ tablespoon Worcestershire sauce
$^1/_3$ cup horseradish
$^1/_2$ teaspoon lemon juice
$^1/_4$ teaspoon dry granulated garlic

MIX ALL INGREDIENTS well and refrigerate. **Makes 2 cups.**

Smoked Corn Relish

1 quart tomatoes, peeled and diced
1 yellow onion, diced
4 jalapeño peppers, minced
3 pounds sweet cut corn
1 red onion, diced

COMBINE ingredients in baking pan and place in smoker, stirring occasionally.

☛ You've got to smoke some things if you're ever going to really experience the Southwestern taste. Jimi Hendrix said something similar. I can't quite remember.

TURKEY GRAVY

Drippings from roasted turkey
3/4 cup flour
5 cups Turkey Stock (see recipe, page 35)
1 teaspoon sage
1 teaspoon black pepper
1/2 teaspoon salt
Butter (optional)

PUT PAN DRIPPINGS from roasted turkey into a heavy skillet. Add flour and stir well. If this roux is too thick, add a little melted butter. Cook over medium heat about 5 minutes or until flour no longer smells raw. Stir in turkey stock and let cook over medium heat until thickened. Add seasonings and taste. If gravy needs additional thinning, add a little more stock. Correct seasonings and serve with roasted turkey. **Makes about 6 cups.**

CREAM GRAVY

THE LONG VERSION FOR BIG BATCHES:

4 pounds beef bones with marrow
1 cup vegetable oil and bone grease

1 cup flour
2 quarts milk, room temperature
2 teaspoons Worcestershire sauce
2 teaspoons Tabasco Sauce
2 teaspoons black pepper
Salt to taste

ROUX: Brown the bones in a 400° oven for about 2 hours. Remove the marrow and reserve. Reserve the bones for beef stock. Use grease from bones and enough oil to total one cup. Put flour and oil into a 12- or 14-inch cast-iron skillet over medium heat and cook until mixture is the color of butterscotch, about 6 to 8 minutes, stirring constantly. You must not scorch the flour.

GRAVY: Add room-temperature milk slowly, whisking thoroughly to avoid scorching. Add Worcestershire, Tabasco, and black pepper. Cook until milk is absorbed into roux and thickens to the right consistency. Add salt and correct seasonings to your taste. **Makes 2 quarts.**

☛ This is the mother lode, the secret to total Southern flavoring in the kitchen. You can prepare fried chicken, a skillet of white soda cornbread, a bowl of fluffy buttered rice, a bowl of green beans and enough cream gravy to go around in less than an hour and fix a whole bad week at the same time. You can make cream gravy either from bones browned in the oven or in the skillet after making fried chicken or chicken-fried steak.

SKILLET CREAM GRAVY

2 to 3 tablespoons cooking oil
2 to 3 tablespoons flour
2 cups milk, room temperature
Salt, pepper, Worcestershire sauce, Tabasco Sauce, to taste

POUR OFF the cooking oil in your heavy skillet until you only have 2 to 3 tablespoons left. Leave the cracklings. With the heat on medium, sprinkle flour over the oil and whisk them together until you have a golden roux. Add the milk and stir the mixture until it is smooth and starts to thicken. Add salt, pepper, Worcestershire sauce, and Tabasco Sauce to taste. Serve over or under just about anything. **Makes 2 cups.**

☛ This is the gravy you make from the drippings and cracklings from any fried beef, chicken or pork.

BROWN GRAVY

1/2 cup fat from beef and margarine
2/3 cup flour
4 cups beef stock
Beef drippings
1 teaspoon Worcestershire sauce
1 teaspoon black pepper
1 teaspoon Tabasco Sauce
Salt to taste

ROUX: Use fat from cooked roast beef. If insufficient or unavailable, use margarine to make 1/2 cup total. Cook flour and fat or margarine slowly in a heavy skillet, stirring constantly to avoid burning. Cook until medium brown.

GRAVY: Add beef stock, drippings, and seasonings. Stir until gravy thickens to right consistency. Season to taste. Strain through a sieve to improve texture. **Makes 1 quart.**

☛ Deep-down brown and with a stout aroma, this may be the most soulful single item on the menu. At the restaurant we can make a stronger, deeper flavor than is likely at home because we have such a treasure of roast beef scraps left over from our trimmings.

BASS
BASS
LONE STAR
ON TAP
CHOLULA

CHAPTER FOUR

THE MENU

"Every seven-pound fluctuation in the weight of an adult male results in a one-inch fluctuation in his waistline."

—Eli the Tailor

"Anything worth doing is worth doing slow."

—Mike Graham, Old Texas Barbell Company

SINCE THE NATIONAL CRAZE for "low fat" foods began, the American population has steadily increased its girth. Our overweight population has increased from one in four to one in three. As I write this, olestra, a fat substitute, has just been approved by the Food and Drug Administration. It has been widely reported that olestra has deleterious effects on many people, effects that include loss of nutrients and diarrhea. Nowhere has the claim been made that olestra tastes good.

The five-a-day consumption of vegetables and fruits being urged by the folks who gave us the Food Guide Pyramid is a good, conservative nudge in the right direction. What most people need now is a way to punch the proper Pyramid category and have it offer up a wide and delicious variety of foods from all groups in delicious recipes. Five-a-day equals 1,825 servings a year. That is one heck of a lot of servings of vegetables and fruits. Especially if every serving has to be rutabagas or cabbage. Making available a wide variety is the best method of getting anyone to eat a lot of healthy food. A variety of flavors makes less necessary the enhancement of each flavor. And since fat is the best flavor enhancer, followed closely by sugar (even super-premium vanilla ice cream at 25% butterfat is tinkered with by the addition of other fats and sugars), it seems logical that we should use a little of it, spread it around a lot, and mix it up with spices.

Health Food Blues

by Roy Blount, Jr.

I believe in wholesome eating.
Greens, grapes and I agree.
I just think it's self-defeating,

Eating only for tomorrow.
I don't like sliced squash in cornmeal
fried in bacon grease, I love it.
Mama fried it for me, may her aura
Shine, and I decline to rise above it.

If meatloafed to the brim,
You're fuller than if tofu'd.
Health food makes you slim
Because it's narrowly better than no food.

A sample of a five-vegetable plate straight off the Threadgill's menu: black-eyed peas with a bit of onion over rice; carrots, very lightly buttered with a pinch of cloves and sugar; butter beans with bits of ham; and turnip greens flavored with hot peppers and vinegar. Accompanied by a yeast roll or a jalapeño cornbread muffin and a small pat of butter, the meal is huge but the fat content is very low.

The selection of vegetables and salads offered on the Threadgill's menu always exceeds 30. By using just 30 as a base number, the five-vegetable plate is available in 276,432 permutations.

When I choose a vegetable plate I follow a couple of loose rules: Choose no more than one with added dairy products (gravy, mashed potatoes, casseroles), choose no more than one that's fried, choose at least one and usually two that are yellow and/or simply steamed. Always have one salad or a cup of soup.

The oldest advice still turns out to be pretty good. Eat a well-rounded assortment of foods in moderation and get plenty of exercise. Brush your teeth and get plenty of sleep.

SOUPS

The Threadgill family lived in the back of the service station during the war years of the 1940s. It was against the law to sell food without a health department license, which Kenneth didn't have. Restaurants up and down the highway were attracting customers, so Kenneth began to give away soup to satisfy a few regulars who were more interested in wine spritzers and two-for-a-quarter beer than meals.

Scooter Simpson, who lives around the corner, grew up playing with the older Threadgill daughters, Kay and Becky. She says Kenneth's soup was good. She liked it just fine until she finally asked Mrs. Threadgill to tell her, "Just what is an oxtail, anyway?"

I'll wager that if we could dig up the recipe for Kenneth's oxtail soup, we'd have a world record for inexpensive fixings.

You know you have a Southern cookbook in hand when the recipe for vegetable soup begins with three pounds of lean beef. Almost every one of my older cookbooks begins its vegetable soup recipes with beef or beef bones. It's no wonder that my vegetarian friends feel picked on. I have one close friend who really does pick on them, and he says that most of them seem kinda puny. Sure enough, around Momma's kitchen, soups were not usually much in evidence until somebody was ill. Colds and cold weather seem to run together in central Texas. If someone was sick, there would appear some chicken soup in a flash. But if the weather just got real cold, then beef stew or chili was heartier. It seems especially odd that we didn't have more soup when you consider how inexpensively it can be made. I guess it just goes to show another way in which "spare no expense" was applied when it came to the way Momma fed folks.

Poppa said when he was young he could tell how hard times were on his folks by what they had for supper. When things were flush they had chicken and corn on the cob and cornbread for Sunday dinner, and cornbread with lima beans and hocks for supper. When times were bad they had cornbread with plain limas for the noon meal and cornbread with corn soup for supper. To this day he turns down corn in any form.

As the restaurant matured and we became more health-conscious, fresh ingredients and a judicious use of leftovers ("never use anything in soup that doesn't have some sunshine left in it") led to more frequent pots of soup.

Cream of Broccoli Soup

5 pounds fresh broccoli
1 gallon Chicken Stock (see recipe, page 34)
3 ribs celery, chopped in 1/2-inch slices
2 onions, peeled
1 bunch green onions, chopped
10 tablespoons (1 1/4 sticks) butter
4 tablespoons flour
Salt
Pepper
2 bay leaves
Thyme to taste
4 cups half-and-half (or 2 cups milk and 2 cups cream)

TRIM OFF broccoli flowerets and peel the stems with potato peeler. Boil half the broccoli in the chicken stock until tender (about 1/2 hour). In another pan, sauté the celery, onion, and green onions in butter. Add the flour and cook for 10 minutes. Strain the liquid from the broccoli-stock mixture into the sautéed celery and onions. Chop the remaining broccoli into bite-size pieces, add to stock, and simmer for 15 minutes. Add salt, pepper, bay leaves, and thyme. Heat half-and-half, blend into soup, and serve. **Makes about 6 quarts.**

☛ My favorite way to fight a blizzard is to take something really healthy and add cream.

Vegetable Soup

6 tablespoons butter
1/2 bunch celery, chopped
1 large potato, peeled and diced
3 carrots, thinly sliced
1 onion, chopped
4 cups Chicken Stock (see recipe, page 34)
Parsley, minced
Salt
Black pepper

MELT THE BUTTER in a large pot, then add the vegetables. Cook over low heat for about 10 minutes. Add the stock, cover, and simmer for about 30 minutes or until the vegetables are tender. Before serving, add parsley and salt and pepper to taste. **Makes about 5 cups.**

TOMATO SOUP

8 cups tomatoes, peeled, seeded, and diced
3 ribs celery, chopped in 1/2-inch slices
1 large white onion, minced
1 bay leaf
1 teaspoon salt
Dash Tabasco Sauce
Parsley for garnish

PLACE ALL INGREDIENTS except parsley in large saucepan. Bring to a full boil, reduce heat, and simmer 20 minutes. Serve very hot with minced parsley garnish in each cup. **Makes about 2 quarts.**

CORN SOUP

2 cups corn, cut off the cob
1 quart Chicken Stock (see recipe, page 34)
1/2 cup okra, sliced
1 clove garlic, minced
3 ribs celery, chopped in 1/2-inch slices
1 cup cooked chicken, diced
2 teaspoons butter
2 cups hot milk
Parsley for garnish

COOK CORN in chicken stock until tender. Add okra, garlic, celery, and diced chicken. Simmer for about 20 minutes. Add butter, salt, and pepper to taste. Gradually stir in hot milk. Garnish with parsley and serve.

VARIATION: Our Corn off the Cob also makes a wonderful, rich cream of corn soup by blending 2 cups of room-temperature heavy cream to one quart of the recipe after it heats to a simmer. Simmer 2 minutes more and serve.

DRUNKEN BEAN SOUP

3 quarts cooked chili beans and liquid
6 ounces medium beer
2 quarts Vegetable Stock (see recipe, page 36)
4 cups cooked pork, chopped
1½ teaspoons salt
1½ teaspoons black pepper
1 tablespoon Poultry Seasoning (see recipe, page 38)
1 tablespoon chili powder

COOKED VEGETABLE MIXTURE:

4 cups onion, chopped
4 tablespoons margarine
2 cups green bell pepper, chopped

PLACE BEANS in a stock pot with beer and stock and bring to a boil. Add the meat and spices and simmer 30 minutes. Sauté vegetables in margarine until onions are clear, add to beans, and simmer an additional 30 minutes. **Makes 4 quarts.**

SPLIT PEA AND HAM SOUP

4 cups dried split peas
2 quarts hot water
4 quarts Vegetable Stock (see recipe, page 36)

4 cups onion, chopped
4 tablespoons margarine
2 cups green bell pepper, chopped
4 cups cooked ham, chopped
2 tablespoons Poultry Seasoning (see recipe, page 38)
1½ teaspoons salt
1½ teaspoons black pepper

RINSE SPLIT PEAS in cold water. Remove all foreign objects. Soak for an hour in hot water in an 8-quart pot. Bring to a boil and add vegetable stock. Simmer for 1½ hours. Meanwhile, sauté vegetables in margarine until the onions are clear. Add ham, poultry seasoning, salt, pepper, and cooked vegetables to pot. Cook, very slowly, stirring occasionally, until peas begin to break down and the soup begins to stick to pot, a couple of hours. **Makes about 7 quarts.**

TORTILLA SOUP

1 quart Chicken Stock (see recipe, page 34)
1 10-ounce can Rotel extra hot tomatoes
1 avocado, diced into 1-inch pieces
1 large tomato, diced
1 bag tortilla chips

BRING CHICKEN STOCK to a boil, add canned tomatoes, and simmer 20 minutes. To serve, add avocado, fresh tomato, and tortilla chips. **Makes 6 cups.**

☛ This one may be the best example of how wonderful it is to have homemade chicken stock on hand. This soup is as quick as heating the stock, opening one can and one bag of chips, and slicing and dicing the avocado and tomato.

Black Bean Soup

2 cups dried black beans
2 quarts cold water
2 stalks celery, chopped
1 onion, diced
1 ham bone
2 cups cooked ham chunks
1½ teaspoons dry mustard
2 tablespoons lemon juice
Salt and pepper

RINSE BEANS WELL, then soak overnight in cold water. Drain. In an 8-quart stock pot, put soaked beans, 2 quarts cold water, vegetables, and ham bone. Bring to a boil, lower the heat, and simmer for 3 hours until beans are tender, adding water if necessary. Remove the ham bone and discard. Mash beans roughly with potato masher. Add the cooked ham to beans and season with mustard, lemon juice, salt, and pepper. Serve with white rice. **Makes about 5 quarts.**

☛ The only thing hard about this is to remember to soak the beans the night before. If a blue norther sneaks up on you, this soup can be hurried up by using canned beans.

Cold Tomatillo Soup

3 pounds fresh tomatillos, cleaned
2 large onions, sliced
4 cloves garlic, minced
4 jalapeño peppers, seeded and minced
6 tablespoons olive oil
2 cups orange juice
2 teaspoons salt
2 teaspoons ground cumin
3 cups buttermilk
12 cherry tomatoes, halved and seeded

PUT TOMATILLOS in large saucepan. Cover with water. Bring to a boil, then simmer for 10 minutes. Add onions, garlic, and peppers. Cook 2 minutes. Purée all ingredients, except buttermilk. Mix in buttermilk. Chill. Serve very cold garnished with cherry tomatoes. **Makes about 1½ quarts.**

☛ Southwestern flavor, hot and spicy and cold all at the same time. Kinda like our weather on occasion.

SALADS

One night, very late, after I sneaked out of my parents' house to roam the streets wishing I was old enough to drive a car, a kid named Ned Tucker came running down Guadalupe like Paul Revere.

"Elvis is at Lockhart's! Elvis is at Lockhart's!" he screamed as he ran past me without slowing down. Lockhart's was a drive-in ice-cream joint about a block away. I ran about a hundred yards real fast before I got winded enough to snap to my senses and slow down.

Why would Ned Tucker be running away from Lockhart's if Elvis was still there? When I walked up, the place was still buzzing. Sure enough, Elvis had driven through the joint in a Cadillac convertible with a couple of Army buddies just minutes before. He was evidently on leave from Fort Hood, the army base just up the highway from Austin. After all the excitement died down, I made my way back up the street to the Somewhere Stand. The Somewhere Stand was famous for its gigantic burgers, "Some Burgers," and all that running had really worked up a hunger. But when I searched my pockets, I came up short. Since I didn't have 35 cents for a burger, the cook suggested a Frito Salad, which only cost a dime.

I was more than a little puzzled. I hardly ever ate salads in those days, and I would never think of ordering one in a restaurant. Seldom was one of the three vegetables in the meat and three format a salad unless it was potato salad, coleslaw or a wedge of lettuce. But I was hungry and a dime was all I had. So I bought my first restaurant salad.

The fry cook put a nickel bag of Fritos on the cutting board and smashed it with his palm. Then he stood it on edge and slit the other edge open with a knife. He tossed in some shredded lettuce, diced onion and tomato. Then he picked up a Tabasco bottle and glugged it several times into the bag and stirred it all together. It was wonderful.

My understanding of salads hadn't made much progress by the time we opened Threadgill's. If it hadn't been for Roger Swanson, Threadgill's first chef, I probably would have put Frito Salad on the menu. The only other salad I knew how to make was a wedge of iceberg with dressing. And my ideas about dressing were pretty primitive, too. Right on the jar of Miracle Whip, it stated that it was a salad dressing, and since I came across this information in the formative years when I was first learning to read, I just always assumed that it was true.

My naïve notions weren't helped much by the attitude of my family. My Uncle Oscar explained to me that since lettuce had no taste and was supposed to be good for us, we had to put something on it that was not so good for us so that it would taste good enough to eat.

Perhaps the biggest change in my diet as well as in Threadgill's menu over the years has been the addition of salads to almost every meal instead of just those at family reunions and holidays. Serving salads is a fine old Southern tradition, but was only practiced when we gathered in large numbers and had more than we could eat of everything from salads to desserts. Since the motto at Threadgill's is "Every Day Is Thanksgiving!" our salads have become a tradition themselves. I had to make calls from San Antonio to Baton Rouge to Poplarville to gather every aunt's contributions in order to build our salad menu. Here are some of our favorites.

TOSSED SALAD MIX TIP: I've discovered that very few people who do not have their own gardens know that fresh mustard greens have a very hot mustard taste when eaten raw. No kidding. Give it a try. I prefer them to lettuce in my salads and on sandwiches.

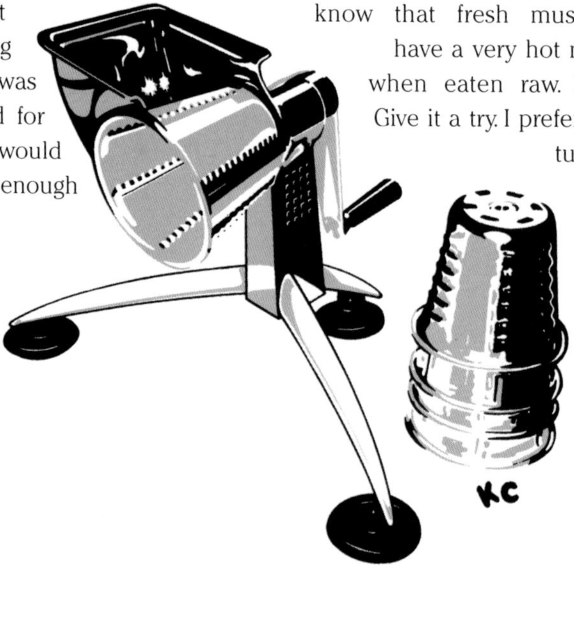

CARROT AND RAISIN SALAD

12 medium carrots, washed and peeled
2 cups raisins
1 tablespoon grated lemon peel
1 tablespoon lemon juice
$^{1}/_{2}$ teaspoon powdered sugar
$^{3}/_{4}$ teaspoon salt
1 cup mayonnaise
1 cup pecans, chopped (optional)

GRATE CARROTS coarsely. Add other ingredients and mix well. Refrigerate. **Makes about 8 servings.**

☛ This is one of the first things I learned to make when Momma got her Salad Master. She decided that she needed to feed us healthier, and with this new gadget I could help without the risk of cutting my little fingers.

BROCCOLI/CAULIFLOWER SALAD

1 bunch broccoli
1 head cauliflower
1 red bell pepper, diced
2 to 3 green onions, chopped
Vinegar and Oil Dressing **(see recipe, page 44)**

CUT BROCCOLI and cauliflower flowerets from stems and steam or blanch until very slightly softened. Cool and add bell pepper and green onions. Toss with Vinegar and Oil Dressing just before serving.

☛ Don't make more of this healthy and delicious dish than you plan to eat at one meal. It doesn't hold well.

COLESLAW

SLAW DRESSING:

3 cups mayonnaise
4 tablespoons cider vinegar
4 tablespoons sugar
1/3 teaspoon white pepper
1/2 teaspoon caraway seeds

CABBAGE MIX:

1 large head green cabbage, sliced very thin
1/2 head red cabbage, sliced very thin
2 carrots, peeled and grated
1 red onion, grated

MIX SLAW DRESSING well and refrigerate. Prepare vegetables and store separately until ready to serve. Rinse the red cabbage and carrots three or four times in cold water to prevent pink and purple discoloration in salad. Mix thoroughly, add dressing, and mix well. **Makes 10 servings.**

☛ By substituting low-fat or no-fat mayonnaise and swapping 1 or 2 cups of Jalapeño Honey Mustard dressing for 1 or 2 cups of mayonnaise, this old standby can be a reduced-calorie treat and a great way to eat some cabbage.

COTTAGE CHEESE AND CUCUMBER

1 quart cottage cheese
2 cucumbers, peeled, seeded, and diced in 1/2-inch pieces
1 tablespoon parsley, chopped
2 green onions, chopped
1/2 teaspoon black pepper
1 teaspoon Tabasco Sauce

MIX ALL INGREDIENTS and refrigerate. **Makes 6 servings.**

☛ By using low-fat or no-fat cottage cheese you can easily create a great addition to anyone's diet repertory.

FRENCH QUARTER PASTA SALAD

- **1 cup black olives, sliced**
- **1/4 cup green chilies, diced**
- **1 red onion, sliced**
- **1/2 cup celery, finely diced**
- **1/2 cup cauliflower, diced**
- **2 teaspoons parsley, minced**
- **1/2 cup mushrooms, thinly sliced**
- **1 teaspoon garlic, minced**
- **2 tablespoons red wine vinegar**
- **1 teaspoon basil leaves**
- **1/2 cup green olives, sliced**
- **1 teaspoon capers**
- **1 green bell pepper, sliced**
- **1/2 carrot, diced small**
- **1/2 cup broccoli, diced**
- **1/4 cup olive oil**
- **1 teaspoon leaf oregano**
- **1 teaspoon tarragon leaves**
- **1/2 cup Vinegar and Oil Dressing (see recipe, page 44)**
- **1 teaspoon black pepper**
- **4 pounds uncooked pasta spirals, fresh or frozen**

MIX ALL INGREDIENTS except pasta. Let stand for 12 hours in refrigerator. Cook and chill pasta. Mix with vegetables and serve as salad or as base for entrée salads. **Makes about 16 servings.**

☛ This is based on the famous muffuletta olive salad. Make a big jar. Use it this week in the pasta salad and next week in the Bronzed Sirloin Pasta Salad.

GREEN BEAN SALAD

2 pounds fresh green beans
1 cup green onions, sliced, tops and all
1 cup red bell pepper, diced
$^1/_2$ cup unsweetened apple juice
4 tablespoons cider vinegar
1 teaspoon black pepper
$^1/_4$ teaspoon oregano

WASH, TRIM, AND CUT green beans. Put 1 inch of water in a large pan and bring to a boil; add green beans. Cook for 5 to 8 minutes. Drain. Combine the beans with all other ingredients. Cover and chill in the refrigerator overnight. **Makes 10 to 12 servings.**

TEXAS CAVIAR

2 quarts canned black-eyed peas, drained
$^1/_2$ cup green bell pepper, diced
2 teaspoons garlic, minced (1 teaspoon is enough for some folks)
1 cup yellow onion, diced
1 cup red onion, diced
1 cup Vinegar and Oil Dressing (see recipe, page 44)
1 tablespoon Vegetable Seasoning (see recipe, page 39)

MIX ALL INGREDIENTS well and marinate 8 to 12 hours, stirring a few times to coat all ingredients well. **Makes 2½ quarts.**

☛ Cowpeas into caviar. Anything is possible in Texas. This simple dish proves the perfection of canned black-eyed peas. The onion and bell pepper provide a delicate crunch, the vinegar a slight tang. For picnics, diets, our Three Salad Lunch Special or good luck on New Year's Day, you really ought to get enough practice on this one to make it easy and frequent.

POTATO SALAD

3 eggs, hard-boiled and grated
4 pounds potatoes, cut in 1-inch chunks
1/2 red onion, chopped
1 tablespoon parsley, chopped
1/3 cup pimiento
1 cup celery, chopped
2 1/2 tablespoons sweet relish
2 1/2 tablespoons mustard
1 1/3 cups mayonnaise
1 teaspoon Tabasco Sauce
1/3 cup Creole mustard
2 tablespoons cider vinegar
1/2 tablespoon white pepper
1 teaspoon salt

HARD-BOIL EGGS and cool. Boil diced potatoes about 15 minutes or until done. Meanwhile, prepare and mix other ingredients. Drain all water from cooked potatoes and mix thoroughly with other ingredients while still hot. Refrigerate uncovered in a shallow dish to cool, then serve. **Makes 3 quarts.**

☛ I like my potato salad with Zatarain's Creole mustard and I like my potatoes very tender.

AMBROSIA

5 large navel oranges, peeled and cut into small pieces
½ cup sugar
1½ cups shredded coconut
½ cup pecans, chopped (optional)

BLEND thoroughly but gently. **Makes 10 servings.**

☛ The secret to perfect ambrosia is to thoroughly peel the oranges. The bitter white membrane is difficult to remove totally but its absence is key. A big jar of ambrosia in your picnic cooler substitutes well for genius.

CHERRY COLA JELL-O™

3 cups cherry juice
2 3-ounce packets black cherry gelatin
3 cups cold cola
1 cup pecans
1 cup cream cheese
2 cups cherries
Leaf lettuce

BOIL CHERRY JUICE and add to gelatin. Stir until dissolved, about 2 minutes, and add cola. Add pecans, cream cheese, and cherries. Chill in a flat 9x13-inch dish until set. Cut into squares and serve on leaf lettuce.

☛ Don't be a snob. Do this one for the kids and you will be thanked a thousand times. It is great for family gatherings because it can be done ahead of time.

BAKING: OUR BREAD AND BUTTER

When Threadgill's opened, I vowed not to serve commercially produced bread if I could possibly avoid it. I knew that bread and gravy, made from scratch, would go a long way toward setting us apart from any other restaurant in what was then an ultra-modest price range. In the beginning and for several years we served nothing but cornbread, baked in sheet pans and cut into large blocks. For a couple of years it was served with wedges of butter sliced by waitresses from one-pound blocks.

Many times I saw slabs of butter as big as the cornbread piece itself rushing toward the dining room. This couldn't possibly work. Obviously, we were throwing away a fortune in butter. But oh, the rave reviews!

The customers loved the cornbread. They loved the obviously real butter, and, of course, they loved the absurd portions. I tried to cajole the wait staff into being reasonable, to cut civilized little pats of butter. Boy, was I dreaming. When the restaurant booms, when the customers are crowded so thick you've got to yell, "Hot food coming through!", reason goes out the window.

Finally, while browsing in Sam Shanblum's restaurant supply store, I spied a device for cutting blocks of butter into little pats, a cute little contraption with neatly secured tiny wires in uniform rows and a lever for pushing them through our one-pound butter blocks. Wow, what a neat machine for only five dollars! I calculated that it would save close to 500 dollars a week in butter waste.

What I didn't calculate was how easy it turned out to be to break the tiny wires. We were always in a hurry, and the tender loving care that we gave the food and the customers never extended to equipment. The effort to use the butter cutter lasted much longer than it would have because of my dad Woody. From the music store down the street he acquired guitar E strings and then piano wire and twice a week for several months he hunkered down and, whistling while he worked, restrung our new little aggravation. We began to think of it as the butter harp. We played our harp, broke the strings, restrung, played and restrung, but never quite got it tuned up just right. In the end I gave up, and the waitresses went back to their big slabs of butter.

In the years following our cornbread-only format, Threadgill's has moved with the times. People are more interested in breads these days. So we have added half a dozen new breads to our daily baking schedule. Nowadays, we set a platter crammed full of fluffy biscuits, steamy yeast rolls, fresh warm slices of homemade wheat or white bread, slabs of cornbread and jalapeño corn muffins on every table.

Other restaurants and groceries have also become more bread-conscious. But it seems that most of what passes for fresh-baked bread these days, even in restaurants that claim to be bakeries, is actually produced from frozen dough trucked in from some national chain headquarters. The difference between our little joint and the rest is where we start. From scratch.

That and the fact that we still serve our bread with way too much butter. Whether our customers actually use it or just leave it on the butter plate, they seem to like the fact that no matter how hard I've tried to talk them into it, our waitresses will not be stingy with the butter.

SOUTHERN CORNBREAD

4 cups corn meal
2 cups unbleached flour
1/3 cup sugar
2 1/4 teaspoons salt
1/3 cup baking powder
6 large eggs
4 cups milk
1 1/3 sticks margarine, melted

PREHEAT OVEN to 350°. Combine corn meal, flour, sugar, salt, and baking powder in a mixing bowl. Whisk in eggs and milk, blending well, and then whisk in the melted margarine. Coat an 11x17-inch pan liberally with nonstick spray or pour in just enough vegetable oil to cover the bottom and rub it up on the sides of the pan. Put the pan in the oven until it is hot enough to cause the batter to sizzle when it is poured into the pan. Bake at 350° for 30 to 35 minutes or until cornbread is set in the center and has begun to pull away from the sides of the pan. Serve hot from the oven or at room temperature. **Makes 24 servings.**

☛ This is the restaurant version of "sheet pan" cornbread.

JALAPEÑO CORN MUFFINS

2 cups corn meal
1 cup unbleached flour
8 teaspoons sugar
1 teaspoon salt
8 tablespoons baking powder, generous
3 large eggs
2 cups milk
6 tablespoons margarine, melted
1/2 cup whole kernel sweet corn
4 tablespoons jalapeño pepper, minced

PREHEAT OVEN to 350°. Combine corn meal, flour, sugar, salt, and baking powder in a mixing bowl. Whisk in the eggs and milk and then add melted margarine, whisking well to blend. Stir in corn and peppers. Spray muffin tins with nonstick spray and fill tins about ⅔ full with batter. Bake at 350° for about 20 to 25 minutes or until muffins are golden brown and have pulled away from the sides of the pan. Cool a few minutes and then turn muffins out of pans. **Makes 18 muffins.**

☞ These little cuties are full of surprises. Cut in two like a biscuit and placed in a bowl of soup, gumbo, or chili, they hold together and contribute to every spoonful. We use our Corn off the Cob in this recipe. It's a little sweeter and the red peppers are pretty.

AUNT ONIE'S WHITE SODA CORNBREAD

2 cups Martha White corn meal
½ teaspoon soda
¾ teaspoon salt
1 tablespoon baking powder
1½ cups buttermilk

PREHEAT OVEN to 450°. Grease a 9-inch cast-iron skillet and preheat skillet in oven. Measure meal, add remaining ingredients, and stir until smooth. (I add a little water to make it a bit soupy.) Pour into very hot skillet. The sizzle you hear when the batter hits the skillet is the sound of the crispy bottom and edges beginning to form. Bake for 25 minutes or until golden brown. Cut in wedges. **Makes 6 to 8 servings.**

☞ When Mother took over the cooking for the family of nine at age 11, Aunt Onie was six years old and Momma's chief assistant. Onie is tucked away in Poplarville, Mississippi, just 13 miles from Lumberton, where they grew up. Today, when you drop in unannounced for a visit, you'd best be hungry. In less time than it takes to say, "No, really, we just ate!" she'll have her long table covered with pot roast, fried chicken, white soda cornbread, cream gravy, brown gravy, rice, potatoes, greens, beans, tomatoes, pecan pie, coconut layer cake. It just doesn't seem to make sense, but Onie makes it seem so easy. She glides around the kitchen like a young ice skater, smiling and joking and answering our questions about her huge garden. Sure enough, a couple of neighbors drop by in the nick of time, then cousin Chuck and a couple of Onie's favorite grandsons. Before you know it, bowls and platters are being stacked in the sink and she's asking what would everyone like for supper. Everything she puts on the table beats any restaurant I've tried so far. Her garden is as big as the Threadgill's parking lot.

Her white soda cornbread is unusual. It's not often you see white cornbread anymore. Cut like pieces of pie from her round cast-iron skillet, it maneuvers well on a plate full of things that accompany gravy.

CORNBREAD DRESSING

8 tablespoons (1 stick) butter
1 medium onion, diced
1 cup celery, diced
1 clove garlic, minced
2 quarts cornbread, crumbled crumbled
2 quarts whole wheat bread crumbs
1 tablespoon sage or Poultry Seasoning (see recipe, page 38)
1 teaspoon thyme
1 teaspoon paprika
1 tablespoon celery salt
1 teaspoon white pepper
2 eggs
1 quart Chicken or Turkey Stock (see recipe, page 34)

PREHEAT OVEN to 350°. Sauté onion, celery, and garlic in butter. Combine cornbread, bread crumbs, and spices. Add sautéed vegetables. Beat eggs into chicken stock and work into bread mixture. Oil casserole. Bake for 90 minutes, covered. **Makes 12 big servings.**

☛ When we serve turkey and dressing at the restaurant, Cornbread Dressing gets put up on the Specials Board as a vegetable. It gets ordered as a side dish by armies of customers who order entrées other than the turkey. It qualifies as a stand-alone Southern comfort food.

THREADGILL'S BISCUIT MIX

1 pound unbleached flour
3 tablespoons sugar
1 teaspoon baking soda
1 teaspoon salt
2 tablespoons baking powder

COMBINE INGREDIENTS in a large, dry bowl and mix thoroughly. **Makes 1 recipe biscuits or shortcakes.**

BUTTERMILK BISCUITS

1 1/4 cups buttermilk
3 tablespoons whipping cream
1/4 cup melted vegetable shortening
3 tablespoons margarine, melted
3 1/3 cups Biscuit Mix (see recipe, above)
2 tablespoons butter, melted

PREHEAT OVEN to 350°. Combine the buttermilk, cream, melted shortening, and margarine. Put the biscuit mix in a mixing bowl and make a well in the center. Pour the liquid into the well and gently mix the wet and dry ingredients together until you have a sticky ball of dough. On a lightly floured surface, roll or pat the dough into a rectangle about half an inch thick and cut with 3-inch biscuit cutter or a glass. Place biscuits on a flat pan lined with baking paper or foil and bake at 350° for about 20 minutes. Rotate the pan during cooking to ensure even browning. Remove from oven when biscuits are golden brown and brush tops with melted butter. Serve with butter, honey, jam, preserves, cane syrup, or cream gravy for breakfast. **Makes 16 3-inch biscuits.**

☛ Gosh, what to say? A perfect one, warm and buttered, should be eaten instead of talked about. Gravy, preserves, sausage, whatever you choose to add to the second and third should not distract from the first. Just butter and a moment of silence. Thank you, Lord.

YEAST ROLLS

6 cups flour
1 tablespoon baking powder, scant
1½ teaspoons salt
¼ cup plus 1½ teaspoons sugar
¼-ounce package dry yeast
1⅞ cups warm water (110°)
1¼ cup vegetable oil, such as canola
1 large egg plus 1 egg yolk

COMBINE FLOUR, baking powder, salt, and ¼ cup sugar in the bowl of a mixer with a dough hook and mix on low speed for 1 minute. Combine yeast and remaining sugar in a small bowl and cover with the warm water. Set aside for a few minutes until the yeast begins to look foamy on top. Whisk together 1 cup of oil with the egg and egg yolk and add to the yeast and water. Add the liquid to the dry ingredients in the mixer bowl and mix on low speed until the dry ingredients are moistened. Turn the mixer off, scrape down the sides of the bowl, and then knead on medium speed for about 5 minutes, adding a little flour if necessary to form a ball of dough. When dough is smooth and elastic, add remaining ¼ cup of oil and knead only to incorporate it into the dough ball. Remove the dough to a well-oiled bowl and cover with plastic wrap. Refrigerate for at least 2 hours or overnight until the dough has doubled in bulk. When the dough has doubled in bulk, punch it down and divide it into 24 pieces (about

2¼ ounces each) and place in well-oiled muffin tins. Cover loosely and allow to double in size again. During the rising time, preheat oven to 350°. Bake the rolls for 15 minutes or until crispy and golden. Cool for about 10 minutes and turn out of pans. **Makes two dozen rolls.**

VARIATION: Add to recipe ½ cup grated cheddar cheese, diced red bell peppers, or sautéed onions.

☛ These little treasures are good at holding their heat deep inside. When you pull them apart a little puff of steam poofs out, looking for butter to melt.

HOMESTYLE WHITE BREAD

10 cups unbleached flour
⅓ cup sugar
⅓ cup nonfat dry milk powder
3 tablespoons dry yeast
1 tablespoon salt
3 cups warm water (110°)
3 tablespoons vegetable oil
Egg wash (1 egg beaten with 1 tablespoon of water)

COMBINE DRY INGREDIENTS in the bowl of a mixer with a dough hook and mix well. Add the warm water and oil and mix on low speed to moisten dry ingredients. Increase the mixer speed to medium and knead for about 4 minutes. Extra flour may be needed at this point to keep dough from sticking to the sides of the bowl. When dough is smooth and elastic, remove to a well-oiled bowl, cover loosely with a clean cloth, and allow to double in bulk in a warm, draft-free place for about 1½ hours. Punch the dough down and divide in quarters. Place dough into 2 greased 4x8x3-inch loaf pans, cover loosely, and allow to double in bulk again. Toward the end of the rising time, preheat oven to 350°. Bake loaves about 25 minutes, then brush tops with egg wash and return to oven for 20 minutes or until loaves are brown on top and sound hollow when thumped on the bottom. Turn loaves out of pans and cool before slicing. **Makes two 1½-pound loaves.**

☛ We make white bread and wheat bread loaves from scratch for our B.L.T., Grilled Cheese, Ham, and Hot Roast Beef sandwiches.

WHOLE WHEAT BREAD

2 1/4 cups whole wheat flour
2 1/4 cups unbleached flour
2 1/2 teaspoons dry yeast
1 1/2 teaspoons salt
1/4 cup vegetable oil
2 tablespoons honey, scant
1 7/8 cups water
2 tablespoons margarine, melted (to brush loaves)

PUT ALL INGREDIENTS except margarine into the bowl of a mixer with a dough hook. Mix at low speed for a few minutes just to moisten dry ingredients and then knead for about 5 minutes on medium speed with the dough hook. Extra flour may be needed to keep the dough from sticking to the sides of the bowl. When dough is smooth and elastic, remove to a large, oiled bowl and cover with a cloth. Allow to rise until doubled in bulk in a warm, draft-free place, about 1½ hours. Punch the dough down and divide into two loaves and place into 2 4x8x3-inch greased loaf pans. Cover the loaves and allow to rise until dough is 2 finger widths above the edge of the pans. During the rising time, preheat oven to 350°. Bake for about 35 minutes or until there is a hollow sound when the loaves are thumped on the bottom. Brush tops of loaves with melted margarine. Turn out of pans and cool loaves before slicing. **Makes two 1½ pound loaves.**

Alka-Seltzer
Prescriptions
Butterfinger
Baby Ruth

Budweiser
LONE STAR

EAT YOUR VEGETABLES!

An old-fashioned Southern restaurant where you could satisfy a serious appetite for very little money was the original idea behind Threadgill's. The idea of serving heaping plates of comfort food with free second helpings was a restaurant concept that went against every low-fat, health-food, vegetarian trend of the era. We figured the health food nuts and dieters would boycott the place anyway. But that's not how it worked out.

I would be a genius if I'd planned it that way, but the truth is it was a complete accident that Threadgill's became known for vegetables. Like any old-fashioned Southern cook, I put either bacon or cheese or butter in almost all our vegetable dishes. Since every other restaurant in the world was trying to cater to health-conscious consumers by serving awful, bland, naked, undercooked steamed vegetables, our customers went crazy for ours because they tasted sensational.

From the beginning, Threadgill's was flooded with people who went wild about our huge vegetable selection. They were ordering plates of three and four vegetables for dinner. I didn't expect it, but when I thought about it I realized how much sense it made. Even if you are on a serious diet and are planning to eat nothing but vegetables, you might as well eat as many as you can when you have the rare opportunity to choose from so many.

If you think about it, a plate full of vegetables made with a little pork fat or butter and some fresh cornbread on the side is just about exactly what the whole food pyramid thing is all about. It's okay to have butter, cream and meat; it's just that you aren't supposed to eat much of them. It's not the bad stuff we *do* eat that causes most of our problems. It's the good stuff we don't eat. So if we fill up at the bottom of the pyramid, we don't have room to eat too much off the top.

Well, the long and short of it is that

the food pyramid that I spent so much time ignoring was part of the reason for our success. The same low-fat consciousness that had more or less killed Southern cooking was also the reason that people couldn't get enough of our Southern-style vegetables.

"Eat Your Vegetables!", the phrase my momma spent so much time preaching to her nursery school kids, became Threadgill's unofficial motto. Back before the pyramid, Momma hung posters on the nursery-school walls showing the basic food groups. But she figured out a long time ago that if she cut up ham in the frozen limas and put brown sugar, vinegar and ketchup in the beans, kids would eat a lot more vegetables.

Once upon a time, Southern cooks put a little pork neck in the collard greens or ketchup in the beans because vegetables were all the *food* they could afford. Today, we are coming full circle. We are eating vegetables seasoned with a little meat because that's all the *calories* we can afford.

Mrs. Curtis's Cook Book has one brief paragraph in its 1,200 pages that comes closest to summing up what became the cornerstone of Southern vegetable cooking:

> Every vegetable is almost lacking in fat; the legumes have the largest proportion, and they average only three per cent. Therefore, fat in some form is added to every vegetable dish. We beat cream or butter into mashed potatoes, bake beans with a bit of pork on top of them, and pour oil over salads.

We have sometimes broken this rule at Threadgill's in honor of the new food era, but we have maintained it where necessary. Our peas and corn, our broccoli and green beans, are now served without the pork, cream or butter that they once contained. Carrots, an example of the other hand, must have at least a light coating of butter or they don't get eaten. Add a bit of clove, the tiniest bit of sugar and cook them perfectly tender, and zounds! We are credited by every hundredth customer as having the best carrots they've ever tasted.

Up through the '50s it was common for encyclopedic cookbooks to have over 50 recipes listed for potatoes. I guess Fanny Farmer still does. In *Mrs. Curtis's Cook Book* from 1914, a whole chapter of 20-some recipes is included for leftover potatoes. When Delmonico's chef Charles Ranhofer published his monster work, *The Epicurean*, in 1894, he was criticized for revealing secrets of culinary wizardry. Sure enough, Mrs. Curtis leads off her list of leftover potato recipes with "Delmonico Potatoes."

MASHED POTATOES

4 pounds Idaho potatoes, peeled and cut in quarters
12 tablespoons (1½ sticks) butter
2 cups half-and-half, or 1½ cups milk
1 teaspoon salt
1 teaspoon black pepper

BOIL POTATOES until tender. Drain and mash with butter, half-and-half, salt, and pepper. Beat until smooth. Serve with cream, brown, or giblet gravy. **Makes 10 servings.**

☛ There are not many things on the planet that taste better than the mashed potatoes we serve at Threadgill's. Certainly there is nothing easier to eat. For most little children who take their first bite of restaurant food at Threadgill's, that bite is mashed potatoes. Mashed potatoes also prove that just because something is simple it is not necessarily easy. How much simpler could it be to peel potatoes, boil them, pour off the water and put them in a mixer with butter, milk, salt and pepper? Easy? Not when you must do it several times a day, several hundred pounds each day, 365 days a year. Tonnage is always tough, and gravity takes its toll.

In the commissary we have a potato peeler that makes it all possible. It can peel 50 pounds of Idaho potatoes in 5 minutes. Really. It looks like a cross between a 55-gallon steel drum and a desktop electric pencil sharpener. You pour the spuds through a hole in the top and they tumble up and down on a spinning, wavy bottom that has the texture of extra-coarse sandpaper. It buffs off the peelings, which then ooze out of the bottom as mush. We shovel the peelings into barrels for a hog farmer who picks them up daily. Only a couple of feet away from the peeler is the stock pot ring, a huge burner that sits low, close to the floor. Next to it sits an 80-quart mixer with a dolly for wheeling the big pots of potatoes between pieces of equipment. The above recipe is sort of home-size.

NEW POTATOES WITH GARLIC AND GREEN BEANS

5 pounds new red potatoes
6 tablespoons butter
1 tablespoon garlic, chopped
1 teaspoon dill
1 teaspoon thyme
1 teaspoon salt
1 teaspoon black pepper
½ pound French-cut green beans

PREHEAT OVEN to 350°. Cut potatoes into halves or quarters. Melt butter and sauté garlic. Sprinkle seasonings over potatoes, followed by garlic butter. Toss or stir to distribute, and place potatoes in single layer on baking pan. Cover pan and place in 350° oven. After 30 minutes, remove cover and turn potatoes. Cook 20 more minutes, stir in green beans, and cook 10 more minutes. **Makes 10 servings.**

☛ These are as easy as mashed potatoes can be difficult. This recipe is a great way to tend to the modern requirement that every meal have potatoes. At the restaurant we sometimes roast the new potatoes in the smoker and we sometimes just roast the garlic a bit in the smoker and add it halfway through the roasting of the new potatoes. Since these are not a daily menu item we can still play with the recipe by simply calling each blackboard version by a different name. The green beans get stirred in when the potatoes are pulled from the oven. By the time they are served, they are tender enough and still colorful.

Scalloped Potatoes

4 pounds Idaho potatoes, peeled and sliced thin ($^3/_8$-inch)
1 small yellow onion, sliced thin
2 teaspoons salt
1 tablespoon black pepper and 2 teaspoons salt, mixed
1 pound Swiss cheese, diced
2 cups milk
4 tablespoons butter, melted

PREHEAT OVEN to 350°. Grease a large casserole and layer half the potatoes, half the onions, half the salt and pepper mix, and half the cheese. Repeat. Mix milk and melted butter and pour over potatoes. Cover and bake for about 2 hours, until very lightly brown on top. **Makes 10 big servings.**

☛ These are known as the consensus builder. Be careful, consensus can be a dangerous thing. A few years ago, not long after we introduced this recipe at the restaurant, I was approached by two opposing political groups, each wanting me to be their candidate in a race for city council. Without knowing anything about my political philosophy, they each assumed that anyone who could serve something as wonderful as this and offer free second helpings could surely do something to improve the quality of what comes out of city hall. I informed them both that I don't do meetings. I can't sit still long enough to do anything but eat, and I eat real fast.

Yams or Sweet Potatoes Baked or Mashed

☛ Put this one in the fall-down-easy category. Bake in oven till done, about 40 minutes at 350°, cut in half, apply a small pat of butter, or not. Eat. Mother would sometimes coax suspicious young newcomers to her nursery school into trying a baked sweet potato by cutting it in the middle, waiting until it was cooled down, then handing it to them like it was an ice cream cone. "Yum!"they would coo, and more often than not the children would become converts.

At home, just scoop them out of the skin after they are baked and mash them up with butter and a tiny bit of cinnamon. When we mash them at the restaurant it pays to peel them and cook them like Idahos before mashing, because we do 100 pounds at a time and we mash them in the 80-quart mixer.

CANDIED SWEET POTATOES

5 pounds sweet potatoes, peeled and cut in 3/4-inch squares
1/4 cup dark corn syrup
1/4 cup maple syrup
2 tablespoons orange juice
1 cup brown sugar
1 teaspoon ginger
1 teaspoon cinnamon

STEAM, MICROWAVE, or cook the sweet potatoes in boiling water until thoroughly tender. Meanwhile, combine other ingredients in small saucepan and cook over medium heat until thick, while stirring. Pour sauce over sweet potatoes. **Makes 10 servings.**

☛ These are done better at Dookey Chase's in New Orleans than any other place I've tried them. Ours are not nearly as sweet nor so thoroughly candied as Dookey's. Leah Chase could sell hers as a dessert. I have opted to make them less sweet simply because I eat them so often.

Onions, Celery and Garlic: The Holy Trinity of Southern Cooking

The most important vegetables in Southern cooking with the fewest namesake dishes. Onion rings are not on our menu and probably should be. I get mine at Dirty's down on the Drag when I get my annual hamburger fix. Sweet onion and tomato slices were a favorite sandwich combination of Mother's. Virginia's Cafe, Austin's long-lamented "meat and three," used to keep a mason jar full of green onions in water on the table as an edible centerpiece. Creamed onions have pretty much gone the way of all things creamy. Testimony to the importance of the flavor of onion is the enormous percentage of recipes that include them. Their strength is the reason breath fresheners were big business in this country even before the explosion in popularity of pizza and garlic.

My friend who imitates W. C. Fields every waking moment calls celery the chewing gum of the aerobics crowd and claims that it is promoted secretly by the dental floss industry. It is probably the only natural food, except maybe for carrots, that's almost as well known for the sound it makes when eaten as for any other property. It has a good moisture content that makes it valuable in cooking. I picture it first with butter, onions and garlic in a cast-iron skillet. Second, with pimiento cheese on a party tray, and third, with peanut butter gripped tightly in the hand of a scared new child in Mom's nursery, her organic pacifier.

> If onion was the aftershave of Momma's cooking, garlic was the cologne.

Garlic is economical, it grows like a weed, and a little goes a long way, so naturally it caught on around our house. A few little cloves stuffed into a pork roast represents the easiest possible way to improve something already near perfect. My Zyliss garlic press makes one clove mix thoroughly with ease into anything from butter or grits to mayonnaise. Poppa used to say, "If onion is the aftershave of Momma's cooking, garlic is the cologne."

Peas, Beans and Such

Santa Fe Succotash

1 pound corn, fresh or frozen
1 pound French-cut green beans
½ cup Chipotle Cream Sauce (see recipe, page 47)
2 15-ounce cans black beans
1 large tomato, diced

Heat the corn and green beans separately. While they are heating, make Chipotle Cream Sauce. Mix corn, green beans, and black beans. Serve topped with diced tomato and Sauce. **Makes about 16 servings.**

☛ An invention for several purposes: For years I've been fond of the way the word "succotash" sounds coming out of my mouth. I guess I was more influenced by Sylvester the Cat cartoons than I realized. I could not, however, find anyone who shared my fascination with the word and I had only encountered one recipe for the dish that caused any excitement. Actually, it was the only recipe I had ever seen served at all. It is simply impossible to get anyone to eat the stuff. That one recipe belonged to a good friend, and it was occasionally his contribution to party fare. He protected the secret for years until he got tired of me badgering him for it. Then he admitted the reason it was so good in spite of having the traditional lima beans and hominy. It was dosed with heavy whipping cream. By the time he coughed up the recipe (it was more like a confession), we were already into this new age of flagrant fat fear. Besides that, the poor holding qualities of cream had already knocked our creamed corn off the restaurant menu. It looked as though succotash had slim prospects for survival in the vocabulary. What a shame. It was supposedly the first recipe given the Pilgrims by the Narragansett Indians. I have even found references to succotash being a frozen dish prepared by the Indians as early as 1620. My vested interest in frozen food was thus threatened by its imminent demise.

But when Mark Miller opened a Coyote Cafe in Austin recently, succotash came back to life for me. You see, Miller ran into heartier eaters here than he'd known before and many of them thought his food was too hot. He got front-page banner headlines to advertise his dilemma and he responded with style and grace. Up until he hit town I had ignored his Southwestern trendiness, but once he became a neighbor it seemed only right to honor his presence with a couple of tips of the hat. We developed our version of what seemed best about his fare: one, a method of preparing a number of our entrées Southwestern style, and two, a really pretty vegetable dish called Santa Fe Succotash.

BLACK-EYED PEAS

1 pound dry black-eyed peas, rinsed
3 quarts cold water
1 cup yellow onion, diced
1 clove garlic, minced
1 green bell pepper, diced
1 teaspoon black pepper
Salt to taste
Thinly sliced onions for garnish
8 strips bacon (optional)

CLEAN, RINSE, and soak peas at least 30 minutes in cold water. Drain and place all ingredients except salt into 4-quart pot. Heat to a boil, then reduce heat and simmer until tender, about 90 minutes. Add additional water as necessary. Add salt to taste and garnish with sliced onion. Add 8 slices of crisp, drained bacon, cut into 1-inch pieces. Put the bacon into the pot 5 minutes before the peas are done cooking. **Makes 12 servings.**

☛ I'm sometimes amazed at what compromises I have made to steer Threadgill's through the choppy straits of public opinion. Not putting bacon in the peas and beans, for instance. If not for the wailing and nagging of dedicated vegetarians I would never have acquiesced to such a notion. Now I find that even my Aunt Onie puts turkey bacon in her peas and greens these days instead of real bacon. She says that Uncle Charles's mouth shouldn't have to make all the adjustments that his heart requires.

Because we serve so many orders of black-eyed peas, 365 days a year, we use dried peas for consistency. Canned peas are too expensive in the quantity we cook. It just represents too many tin cans. Whenever we can find affordable prices with area growers we put "fresh-shelled peas" on the Specials Board and, whether they are purple hulls, crowders, or lady creams, they almost grow wings and fly out the pass-through window.

HOPPING JOHN

☛ Hopping John is another recipe name I want to keep in the vocabulary. I don't know how it got the name, but I love to say it and I love to eat it. It fits perfectly (especially in a vegetarian form) into the new age of healthy considerations, and is simply the combination of black-eyes and rice. The combination of legumes and grains is highly touted as the way to make a whole protein. Served in the traditional red-beans-and-rice manner, with the peas and their liquor filling in an indention in a mound of white rice, it takes on a stature more stately than that afforded the lowly cowpea.

Rice takes 20 minutes to cook. I begin a meal by putting on a pot of water for rice, then I check the big Jax clock on the wall and set about accomplishing as much of a meal as possible in the next 20 minutes. I cook the rice in chicken stock and the peas with ham and serve them with fried chicken, ham steaks, or on a plate with other vegetables and slices of tomato.

FRESH PEAS

$1\frac{1}{2}$ pounds fresh purple hull, crowder, or lady cream peas, rinsed
3 quarts cold water
1 cup yellow onion, diced
1 teaspoon dry mustard
1 teaspoon black pepper
$\frac{1}{4}$ pound bacon, cooked and diced
$\frac{1}{2}$ teaspoon salt
Sliced onion for garnish

CLEAN, RINSE, and drain peas. Place all ingredients except bacon and salt in a 4-quart pot. Bring to a boil, then reduce to simmer. Cook about 60 minutes or until tender. Add bacon, then salt to taste. Garnish with sliced onion and serve. **Makes 10 servings.**

NOTE: This recipe works fine for any fresh peas.

BAKED BEANS

1 gallon canned pork and beans
1 quart ketchup
2 yellow onions, diced
1 green bell pepper, diced
$\frac{2}{3}$ cup brown sugar
$\frac{1}{2}$ cup sweet relish
$\frac{1}{2}$ pound bacon, cooked and diced
2 teaspoons Worcestershire sauce
1 teaspoon Tabasco Sauce
1 teaspoon dry granulated garlic
1 teaspoon white pepper
$\frac{1}{2}$ teaspoon cumin

MIX all ingredients and bake in lightly oiled covered casserole dish at 350° for 1 hour.

VARIATION: Mince 3 or 4 nice hot jalapeño peppers and add to mix to create spicy Austin Baked Beans.

☛ There is a difference between having no secrets and telling everything. Some things just seem not to get talked about all that much. Pork and sugar as seasoning in vegetables, and canned goods in recipes, are no longer considered politically correct by sophisticated contemporary cookbooks. Baked beans as we prepared them at Momma's nursery school broke all these taboos. Canned pork and beans cannot be outdone by the best efforts as the lead ingredient in this slightly sweet, slightly sticky recipe. Some of the kids just simply ate without breathing till they gasped for air and then went down again till they groaned. They all wanted second helpings, but there was a catch. Momma always tried to serve them rutabagas or cabbage or turnip greens—something with no sugar and not much bacon seasoning, something that they usually didn't care much for. To get seconds on one dish, they had to "clean their plate" of the others.

GREEN BEANS

4 pounds harvester green beans, cut
8 ounces almonds, sliced
2 tablespoons butter
8 ounces bacon, cooked and diced
1 teaspoon salt
1 teaspoon black pepper

SAUTÉ almonds in 1 tablespoon butter and set aside. Steam or boil beans, remove while still crisp, and mix in almonds, bacon, remaining butter, salt, and pepper.

☛ Green beans are typically the biggest hit-and-miss fresh vegetable delivered by purveyors to the restaurant (with the possible exception of watermelon). They may look perfect, snap crisply, seem juicy and tender, yet when they are cooked turn out tough, stringy or tasteless. Poppa says it's because all the good beans get canned; nevertheless, there is no escaping the need to try over and over again, especially at certain times of the year. Pick the best ones you can find, drop in boiling water for a couple of minutes too few, and let them finish tenderizing themselves in a covered dish with the butter, almonds and bacon. When guests exclaim that the beans are perfect and wonder how you did them so perfectly, I mean it when I reply, "Just lucky."

OLD SOUTH BUTTER BEANS

1 pound large dry lima beans
3 quarts cold water or Chicken Stock (see recipe, page 34)
1 ham hock or 1/4 pound ham, diced
1 cup yellow onion, diced
1 teaspoon black pepper
1/2 teaspoon salt
Sliced onion for garnish

CLEAN, RINSE, and soak beans at least 1 hour in cold water. Drain and place all ingredients except salt into a 4-quart pot. Heat to a boil, then reduce heat and simmer for 60 minutes or until tender. Add additional liquid if necessary. If using ham hock, trim meat and return to pot and discard bone. Add salt to taste and garnish with sliced onion. **Makes 10 servings.**

☛ These beans, whether they be limas, baby limas, butter beans or not, need to be cooked tender, need to be gravied together a bit and flavored as thoroughly as possible with mild pork or ham (not smoked) and black pepper. Properly thick and soft, served with hot buttered cornbread, they are among the healthiest of authentic comfort foods.

RED BEANS AND RICE

RICE:

½ pound bacon
1 cup yellow onion, diced
1 green bell pepper, diced
4 ribs celery, diced
1 clove garlic, minced
2 teaspoons Meat Seasoning (see recipe, page 38)
3 cups cold water
1½ cups converted long-grain rice

BEANS:

1 pound large red kidney beans
4 cups Vegetable Stock (see recipe, page 36)
4 cups cold water
2 cloves garlic, minced
1 medium jalapeño pepper
1 teaspoon black pepper
1 bay leaf
¼ pound breakfast sausage
1 cup yellow onion, diced
1 cup celery, chopped
¼ pound bacon, minced
½ teaspoon salt
Sliced green onions for garnish

PREHEAT OVEN to 350°.

RICE: Cook bacon and reserve for beans. Sauté onion, bell pepper, celery, and garlic in bacon fat. Place all ingredients in a covered casserole dish and bake until done, about 45 minutes.

BEANS: Clean and rinse beans. Soak at least 4 hours in cold water to cover well. Drain beans and place in a 2½-quart or larger pot with stock, water, garlic, jalapeño, black pepper, and bay leaf. Bring to a boil, reduce heat to simmer, cover, and cook until beans begin to soften, about an hour. Meanwhile, cook crumbled sausage with onion and celery until onion is well-browned. Add reserved bacon, sausage, celery, and onion to beans. When beans are tender, remove from kettle, add salt if needed, and serve over prepared rice. Garnish with green onion. **Makes 10 servings.**

☛ If the people of the South had no choice but to pick one dish and no other to eat, it is possible that this might be the only thing they would ever agree on—so long as cornbread was part of the bargain.

TEXAS CHILI BEANS

1 pound pinto beans
3 quarts cold water
1 cup yellow onion, diced
1 clove garlic, minced
1/4 cup chili sauce
1 teaspoon chili powder
1 teaspoon black pepper
1 teaspoon cumin
1 teaspoon cayenne pepper
1 teaspoon Tabasco Sauce
1/2 teaspoon salt
Sliced onions for garnish

CLEAN AND RINSE pinto beans. Soak overnight in cold water to cover well. Drain beans and place all ingredients except salt into 4-quart pot and bring to a boil. Reduce heat to simmer. Cover and cook about 90 minutes or until beans are tender. Add salt to taste and garnish with sliced onion. **Makes 2 quarts.**

☛ These are the beans that should never be cooked in the chili. These are the beans that should be added to the chili when there is chili and eaten without the chili on many occasions when there is no chili. Like our black-eyed pea recipe, this is a vegetarian recipe simply because so many vegetarians frequent the restaurant. And after all, our chili recipe is not even slightly vegetarian.

REFRIED BEANS

2 ounces vegetable shortening
½ gallon Chili Beans (see recipe, page 96)
1 tablespoon jalapeño juice
1 or 2 pickled jalapeños, minced
¾ teaspoon cumin
¾ teaspoon Poultry Seasoning (see recipe, page 38)

MELT SHORTENING in large skillet. Add beans and mash with potato masher. Add other ingredients and continue stirring until hot enough to serve. **Makes about 8 servings.**

SNAP PEAS, PEPPERS AND CORN

1 cup yellow onion, diced
1 tablespoon butter or margarine
1 teaspoon garlic, minced
3 cups cold water
1 cup sweet corn
2½ pounds cut green beans
1 cup red pepper, diced
1 tablespoon Poultry Seasoning (see recipe, page 38)

SAUTÉ ONION in butter and add garlic. Add other ingredients, bring to a boil, reduce to simmer, and cook until beans are done, about 30 minutes. **Makes 10 big servings.**

BOILED GREENS

2 pounds fresh or frozen greens
4 cups water
$^1/_2$ pound bacon, cooked crisp and diced
$^1/_4$ teaspoon dry mustard
$^1/_4$ teaspoon white pepper
$^1/_2$ teaspoon salt
1 teaspoon vinegar

IF USING fresh greens, wash thoroughly. Place all ingredients in a 6-quart stock pot. Bring to a boil, reduce heat, cover, and simmer until tender, about 30–40 minutes. Check seasonings, and serve with pepper sauce, etc. **Makes 10 servings.**

☛ A Mess O' Greens, be they spinach, turnip greens, swiss chard, mustard or collard greens. (They are hard to clean thoroughly. A salad spinner is indispensable.) Serve with pepper sauce and onion. Frozen greens are perfectly acceptable, canned greens are perfectly horrible.

BROCCOLI

☛ **Fact:** Fresh broccoli, next to mashed potatoes, has been the most ordered and most praised vegetable on the Threadgill's menu. **Fact:** The first fact is the most amazing surprise of all to me. (Thank you, Roger Swanson, Threadgill's first kitchen manager.) This is how we do it so successfully. First, we trim the broccoli for the largest possible heads on medium-sized stalks. Then we put a hotel pan full of broccoli (about 6 pounds) in the steamer long enough to get it three-quarters done, about 3 to 4 minutes. Then we cool it with cold water and move it to the cooking line where we cover it with ice to retard further cooking and retain its color. The pan has a special place in our cooking line next to the range top, on which is placed a large pot of boiling water and a blanching basket just like the one I use at home. When orders for broccoli are received, we drop the vegetable in the basket. The basket is lowered into the boiling water for a minute, raised and drained, and the broccoli is put on a plate garnished with lemon.

CABBAGE

☛ *Mrs. Curtis's Cook Book* of 1914 has 19 recipes for cabbage. The Culinary Arts Institute cookbook of 1950 has 12 recipes. It says something about the Threadgill's menu that our recipe for Creole Cabbage is the recipe used in a 1993 publication, *Texas Home Cooking*. Nobody else is trying to sell cabbage. (It says something about *Texas* cookbooks published in *Boston* that they chose to drop the "Creole" from our recipe name.)

The morning Sandra and I began to deliver our new line of frozen vegetable chubs, I had my semiannual sighting of a *Wall Street Journal*. In the middle of the front page there was a headline that boldly proclaimed: "CABBAGE, THE PARIAH OF THE VEGETABLE KINGDOM!" The article went on to detail why this year marked the 30th-some annual decline in cabbage sales. With wounded expectations I went about my deliveries knowing that our beautiful Creole Cabbage, bright red in its transparent sausage chub, would probably not survive. Sure enough.

As healthy as it is and as easy as it stir-fries, it would seem that the wok-it scientists of the '80s would have done something to help the cabbage gain popularity. Still, the zillions of daily Poboys that get shredded cabbage instead of lettuce at Mother's in New Orleans would seem to ensure its survival.

My mother just boiled it with onion and ate it with pepper sauce that was mostly vinegar. It was kinda like her penicillin and it may have been her way of reminding us that the Depression might return at any time. Goodness knows it depressed me to come home and raise the lid of a pot on the stove and discover boiled cabbage. Momma cooked it with the lid on till she figured it was done and then, if people had gathered in the kitchen, she walked the pot out to the porch to remove the lid.

Creole Cabbage

6 slices bacon, diced
2 cups yellow onion, diced
4 cups tomatoes, diced
1 head green cabbage, cut into 1¼-inch squares
4 cups tomato sauce
1 cup water
½ teaspoon Tabasco Sauce
½ teaspoon salt
½ teaspoon black pepper

SAUTÉ DICED BACON, add onion, and continue cooking. Add all other ingredients and bring to a boil, stirring to avoid scorching. Turn down to a simmer and stew until cabbage is done, about 1 hour. **Makes 10 big servings.**

Carrots

☛ I think the reputation of the poor carrot was almost destroyed by food purveyors who turned tiny carrot cubes and English peas into the institutional monster hit of the century. Peas and carrots, ah what a clear green-and-orange picture it conjures up for every person who ever went through a school lunch cafeteria several hundred times. Headline I expect to see someday: "Study Finds Peas and Carrots the Most-Served and Least-Eaten Vegetable Dish of Century!"

Baby carrots, sweet and snappy crisp, are the best new healthy edible I've discovered at H-E-B Central Market. They are so sweet and so crisp that they substitute even for peanuts, yet they have no fat. Keep them in a covered bowl of ice water in the fridge when you are suddenly spending all day working around the house. The habit of opening the refrigerator door over and over, absentmindedly looking for a snack, is a hard habit to break, and an even harder habit to feed.

Buttered Carrots

3 pounds sliced carrots or whole baby carrots
4 tablespoons butter
2 teaspoons sugar
1/4 teaspoon cloves
1/4 teaspoon white pepper
Parsley for garnish

Peel or scrub carrots (gunny sack scrubber). Steam, microwave, or cook in boiling water until tender. Melt butter, add seasonings, and coat carrots. Garnish with parsley and serve. **Makes 10 big servings.**

Roasting Ears

☛ If you don't eat a few ears of corn on the cob each year you will not develop your full potential as a human being or ever fully understand the true value of dental floss.

SWEET CORN OFF THE COB

6 cups cold water
1/4 yellow onion, diced
1/2 green bell pepper, diced
1/4 red bell pepper, diced
1 tablespoon Vegetable Seasoning (see recipe, page 39)
2 tablespoons cornstarch dissolved in 1/2 cup cold water
2 pounds sweet kernel corn

IN A 4-QUART pot put water, onion, bell peppers, seasonings, and cornstarch. Boil, reduce to simmer, and add corn. Cook until corn is tender, about 30 minutes. **Makes 8 big servings.**

☛ This recipe was developed specifically for our frozen food line. It is healthy, pretty, easy to fix and works wonderfully as a starter for several other recipes, such as Corn Soup or Creamed Corn Diablo.

CREAMED CORN DIABLO

1 quart Corn Off the Cob (see recipe, above)
4 jalapeños, diced
4 tablespoons butter
4 teaspoons flour
1 cup Mexican sour cream

HEAT Corn Off the Cob recipe with jalapeños. Add butter, flour, and Mexican sour cream. Stir till thickened.

Song to Grits

by Roy Blount, Jr.

When my mind's unsettled,
When I don't feel spruce,
When my nerves get frazzled,
When my flesh gets loose—

What knits
Me back together's grits.

Grits with gravy,
Grits with cheese.
Grits with bacon,
Grits with peas.
Grits with a minimum
Of two over-medium eggs mixed in 'em: um!

Grits, grits, it's
Grits I sing—
Grits fits
In with anything.

Rich and poor, black and white,
Lutheran and Campbellite,
Southern Jews and Jesuits,
All acknowledge buttered grits.

Give me two hands, give me my wits,
Give me forty pounds of grits.

Grits at taps, grits at reveille.
I am into grits real heavily.

True grits,
More grits,
Fish, grits, and collards.
Life is good where grits are swallered.

Grits
Sits
Right.

GARLIC CHEESE GRITS

6 cups cold water
1½ cups hominy grits
¼ cup milk
2 eggs, beaten
1 teaspoon garlic, minced
1 tablespoon yellow onion, minced
8 ounces Velveeta, cubed
½ teaspoon salt

PREHEAT OVEN to 350°. Bring water to a boil. Add grits and return to a boil. Reduce heat and simmer about 5 minutes. Remove from heat, add all other ingredients, and put into oiled casserole pan. Bake covered for about 45 minutes, stirring midway. **Makes 10 big servings.**

EGGPLANT

1 eggplant, peeled and cut into strips or rounds
Salt
Juice of lemon
Flour
Buttermilk
Bread crumbs
Frying oil

CUT EGGPLANT either in 8 to 10 strips or in ½-inch rounds. Salt and rub with lemon juice. Let stand for 30 minutes. Press between paper towels to remove moisture. Roll in flour, dip in buttermilk, roll in bread crumbs. Fry in vegetable oil to cover at 375° for 5 minutes or until golden.

☛ These Guinea melon, or Guinea squash, as they were known originally for their African origin, are highly adaptable for several methods of cooking. I like them fried like little chicken-fried steaks or cut lengthwise like steak fingers. They fit better in a pan cut lengthwise but rounds work well in the New Age rage for eggplant in sandwiches. I like them on a 6-inch Poboy bun with arugula, mustard greens, Jalapeño Honey Mustard and slaw.

Stuffed eggplant is another reason to make a trip to New Orleans. But that's another story!

CAJUN-ITALIAN EGGPLANT

4 tablespoons butter or margarine
2 cups yellow onion, diced
$^1/_2$ cup celery, diced
$^1/_2$ cup green bell pepper, diced
1 teaspoon garlic, minced
1 teaspoon jalapeño pepper, minced
4 cups eggplant, peeled and cubed in $^3/_4$-inch pieces
$^1/_2$ cup mushrooms, sliced
1 green onion, chopped
1 pound tomatoes (2 or 3), diced
6 ounces tomato juice
1 teaspoon oregano
$^1/_2$ teaspoon basil
1 teaspoon Vegetable Seasoning (see recipe, page 39)
$^1/_2$ cup crumbled crackers
Parsley for garnish

PREHEAT OVEN to 350°. In a large skillet sauté onion, celery, bell pepper, garlic, and jalapeño in butter. Remove from heat and mix with eggplant, mushrooms, green onions, diced tomatoes, tomato juice, oregano, basil, and seasoning. Place in oiled casserole dish and sprinkle crackers on top. Cover and bake for 1 hour. Garnish with parsley and serve. **Makes 10 big servings.**

☛ If you like eggplant you should prepare this recipe—now.

OKRA

Here is a vegetable that stirs feelings as strong as those on either side of the chili and BBQ arguments. Some call okra slick and slimy, the squid of the vegetable kingdom. Hybrids have been developed to reduce this property, but purists find the original texture perfect. Probably most people know all they want to about okra. The fact that it was smuggled into this country by African slaves who hid the seeds in their hair is testimony to the strength of its cultural importance.

Nowadays, most who eat it eat it fried. Pickled okra is about as good as anything you can pickle and better than some, such as watermelon rind. A semi-local Cajun friend, a small tall-tale teller who will not stay transplanted, told me of his grandmother's okra roux. When she concocted it as a nearly fat-free, cholesterol-free cooking roux for her heart-ailing husband, his granny was light-years ahead of her time. In a large cast-iron pot she put the tiniest bit of oil and slowly cooked the moisture out of a bit of celery and okra. When she could add a little more okra without it sticking, she would, over and over again, adding as little water as possible until she had several days' worth of goo roux for Granddad's gumbo and étouffée.

Song to Okra

by Roy Blount, Jr.

It may be poor for eating chips with,
It may be hard to come to grips with,
But okra's such a wholesome food
It straightens out your attitude.

Okra's green,
Goes down with ease.
Forget cuisine,
Say "Okra, please."

STEWED OKRA AND TOMATOES

- **1/4 pound bacon, diced**
- **1 cup yellow onion, diced**
- **2 cups tomatoes, diced**
- **1/2 pound frozen cut okra**
- **2 cups tomato sauce**
- **1/2 cup water**
- **1/2 teaspoon Tabasco Sauce**
- **1/2 teaspoon salt**
- **2 teaspoons black pepper**
- **1–2 cups corn kernels (optional)**

SAUTÉ DICED BACON, add onion, and continue cooking. Add all other ingredients and bring to a boil. Reduce to a simmer and stew, stirring occasionally, for 45 minutes or until okra is tender. **Makes 10 big servings.**

☛ When I make myself a Three, Four, or Five Vegetable Plate at the restaurant, I use several criteria in the selection process. Color is one. I classify our Stewed Okra, the Creole Cabbage and the Cajun-Italian Eggplant as red dishes. You've gotta see 'em to believe 'em. They're gorgeous!

YELLOW SQUASH

- **4 tablespoons butter**
- **1 cup yellow onion, thinly sliced**
- **1 cup Chablis**
- **4 pounds yellow squash (about 10 or 12), sliced about 1/2-inch thick**
- **1 teaspoon Worcestershire sauce**
- **1 teaspoon Tabasco Sauce**
- **1 teaspoon white pepper**
- **Parsley for garnish**

IN A HEAVY 14-inch skillet, melt butter and sauté onions. Add wine, squash, and seasonings. Cook over medium heat, turning squash until all is cooked. Garnish with chopped parsley. **Makes 8 big servings.**

☛ Here is another color classification. It also fits into a category I think of when I'm deciding on my meatless mountain of morsels: super healthy. No fats to speak of. The tiny bit of butter divided among several servings doesn't amount to much. And talk about pretty on the plate.

CASSEROLES

These casseroles are each examples of how to combine several different food groups into single dishes that are then greater than their parts.

BROCCOLI AND RICE CASSEROLE

RICE:

6 cups converted long-grain rice
3 quarts cold water

CASSEROLE:

2 tablespoons butter or margarine
2 cups yellow onion, diced
1 cup cold water
6 heads broccoli, chopped medium-coarse (use flowerets and softer part of stalk)
2 pounds Velveeta, cut in $^{3}/_{4}$-inch cubes
1 pound water chestnuts, sliced
1 pound mushrooms, sliced
$2^{1}/_{2}$ cups cream of mushroom soup (undiluted)

COOK RICE and set aside. Preheat oven to 350°. In a large skillet melt butter and sauté onion. Add water and broccoli to skillet. Cook over medium heat, stirring occasionally until broccoli is slightly softened, about 5 minutes. Remove from heat and mix in cheese, water chestnuts, mushrooms, cream of mushroom soup, and cooked rice. Place mixture in covered casserole dish and bake for about 25 minutes. Stir and bake 25 more minutes. **Makes 10 big servings.**

SAN ANTONIO SQUASH CASSEROLE

◆

2 tablespoons butter or margarine
2 cups yellow onion, diced
4 pounds yellow squash, sliced 3/8-inch thick
8 ounces Velveeta, cut in 3/4-inch cubes
1 cup cream of celery soup (undiluted)
1 cup green chilies, diced
1/2 cup bread crumbs
Parsley for garnish

PREHEAT OVEN to 350°. In a 14-inch pan, sauté onion in butter. Add squash and cook until slightly softened. Squash will release a lot of water, which must be drained. Mix squash and onion with cheese, soup, and green chilies and place in oiled casserole dish. Cover with bread crumbs and bake about 30 minutes or until hot throughout. Garnish with parsley and serve. **Makes 10 big servings.**

☛ This squash casserole was brought to Threadgill's by a kitchen manager who grew up with it. Variations of it have appeared all over the area since we began to serve it. Santa Fe, San Angelo, San Saba have all been attached to it on blackboards across the plains. We used to rotate our casseroles on different days of the week but we had so many customers who were so devoted, each to their own favorite, that we now serve them each and every day.

SPINACH CASSEROLE

1 cup yellow onion, diced
3 ounces bacon, diced
2 tablespoons butter
2 pounds spinach, chopped
1/2 pound mushrooms, sliced
1 cup cream of mushroom soup (undiluted)
1/2 pound processed Swiss cheese, diced
Juice of 1 lemon, about 1 ounce
1/2 cup crackers, crumbled

PREHEAT OVEN to 350°. Sauté onion with bacon and butter. Mix with all ingredients except crackers and put into oiled casserole dish. Sprinkle with crackers. Cover and bake about 60 minutes. **Makes 10 big servings.**

SPINACH CASSEROLE BILL ARNOLD

5 10-ounce packages frozen chopped spinach
1 pound bacon, fried very crisp
2 onions, chopped, sautéed
1 pound Swiss cheese, grated
Juice of 4 lemons
21 ounces cream of mushroom soup (undiluted)
Salt and pepper to taste
1/2 pound (2 sticks) butter
2 small cans mushroom stems and pieces, drained
Cracker crumbs, if needed for consistency

PREHEAT OVEN to 350°. Cook frozen spinach as directed, drain well. Fry the bacon, sauté the onions, and add remaining ingredients in order listed. Add cracker crumbs if needed to make a fairly stiff mixture. Bake uncovered for 30 minutes at 350°. **Makes about 16 servings.**

☛ This is the single most versatile, perhaps the most wonderful, recipe ever given to me. Thank you, Bill Arnold, you big baritone gourmet. This larger recipe is recommended. The leftovers are just the ticket for preparing about a dozen recipes that are some of the best and easiest in this collection, once you have the Spinach Casserole ready to go.

MACARONI AND CHEESE

1½ cups milk
1 pound Velveeta, cut in ¾-inch cubes
4 tablespoons butter or margarine
½ teaspoon cayenne pepper
½ teaspoon paprika
8 ounces macaroni
4 ounces cheddar cheese, shredded

IN A DOUBLE BOILER, heat milk with Velveeta, butter, and spices. Cook until cheese melts, stirring frequently. Cook macaroni in boiling water until done. Stir frequently to keep from sticking together. Layer macaroni and cheddar in a casserole. Pour the cheese-milk-spices mixture over all. Cover and bake at 350° for 10 to 20 minutes. **Makes 10 big servings.**

☛ Considered by many to be a comfort food group of its own.

VEGETARIAN JAMBALAYA

RICE:

4 tablespoons margarine or butter
$^1/_2$ cup yellow onion, diced
$^1/_2$ cup green bell pepper, diced
2 green onions, chopped
$^1/_2$ teaspoon turmeric
2 cups converted long-grain rice
4 cups Vegetable Stock (see recipe, page 36)

JAMBALAYA BASE:

4 tablespoons margarine or butter
1 quart yellow onions, diced
1 cup celery, diced
2 green bell peppers, diced
2 jalapeños, minced
1 tablespoon garlic, minced
1 cup cauliflower, chopped
$2^1/_2$ pounds tomatoes, diced
1 yellow squash, diced
4 ounces mushrooms, sliced
2 cups tomato sauce
1 teaspoon Tabasco Sauce
1 tablespoon Vegetable Seasoning (see recipe, page 39)
1 cup cherry tomatoes, split
$^1/_4$ cup picante sauce, medium
Green onions for garnish

RICE: Preheat oven to 350°. Melt margarine and sauté onion and bell pepper. Place sautéed vegetables and other ingredients in covered casserole dish and bake in oven until rice is just done, about 45 minutes.

BASE: In heavy 14-inch skillet, melt margarine and sauté onion. Add celery, bell pepper, jalapeño, and garlic, stirring to cook evenly. Add cauliflower and stir again. Add all other ingredients and bring to a boil, stirring. Reduce heat to simmer and cook about 20 minutes. Mix base with rice, garnish with green onions, and serve. **Makes 10 big servings.**

☛ Thanks again, Glenn Bob, for another invention specifically designed to fit a need. Jambalaya kinda sorta translates into "clean out the fridge," and I've never known a Cajun who didn't have pork, seafood or chicken in the fridge. The worst that can be said about the dish is that it smacks of vegetarian chili. It doesn't commit the sin, however, of containing tofu. It is chock-full of wonderful vegetables, it's a bit spicy and, all things considered, it does a fine favor to those seeking something substantial, yet meatless.

Entrées and Value Meals

One Friday afternoon in the mid '70s, I left Houston, took a right at Katy and followed the Hockley cutoff road until I hit 290 where I turned north toward Austin. In Waller, I realized that I'd left my wallet back in the Montrose District. Good Lord, I had no money, not even a driver's license. (I didn't go back and get it. In fact, I didn't return to Houston for 12 years.)

As soon as I realized that I was a broke, illegal driver, my stomach began to growl loud enough to scare a yardful of dogs. I craved a beer and a steak and a pillow on a porch swing like I'd never experienced a craving before. Digging in my jeans and sifting through my ashtray produced two dollar bills and about a dollar in silver. I squinted into the sunset and became a vulture scouting for a value meal.

As I approached a little store I'd passed many times before, I saw for the first time a sandwich board bearing the proud and simple letters: BBQ. Suddenly, I knew how much a big fish must love worms.

Inside, the butcher cases and shelves of an old grocery store sat in the dark. Off to the left were a couple of coin-operated pool tables with plastic Miller Beer lights and in the corner was a clean, brightly lit kitchen separated from me by a crude counter and a dozen strides.

A pretty young woman in tight western wear jumped up and with a look of worried agitation headed me off with a boot-scooting rush toward the kitchen. Over her shoulder to her girlfriend, left holding a cue and a Pearl, she chirped, "I just knew the minute Joe Don left me in charge someone would come in."

"Darlene, he's gotta wash that barbecue smell outta his hair and change outta that apron 'fore y'all go to Weimer. Otherwise every girl at that dance gonna be gnawing on him 'fore y'all hit the floor."

I went kinda blind when the smell of smoke and beer hit me. Then my focus went to the bottle of Pearl that Darlene's friend was holding. It was wet and looked cold. I walked slowly toward the light, trying to digest the menu board. It read by the pound and gave reasonable prices for brisket and pork sausage and custom smoking. I remember that the prices were reasonable enough to make me aware of my poverty. I was going to have to buy small. The menu board continued: Sliced Brisket Sandwich, $1.95, Chopped Beef Sandwich, 95 cents.

Chopped beef sandwiches have a bad reputation. Who knows what kind of fat and gristle and what-all they put in them? Ordering a chopped beef sandwich from someplace was a statement of your faith in them. But I was very hungry and the question now was: Two chopped beef sandwiches and one beer to go, or one chopped beef sandwich and two beers to go? Being a stranger to their methods, I ordered one chopped sandwich and two beers.

Darlene looked around and looked around but couldn't seem to find any chopped beef. "I'm sorry, I'm gonna have to chop some up fresh," she apologized. While I stood there salivating, Darlene pulled out a huge and perfect-looking brisket and started slicing off some juicy-looking hunks. Then she started chopping the lean meat up for my sandwich.

"You know what," I said with my tongue hanging out of my mouth, "make that TWO chopped beef sandwiches and one bottle of Pearl."

Those were two of the best chopped beef sandwiches I ever ate. My "value meal" restored my spirits and my faith in my fellow Americans and eventually inspired me to invent Threadgill's own version of chopped beef. We call ours "meatloaf."

We understand that ordering meatloaf, like ordering a chopped beef sandwich, is the ultimate sign of trust in a restaurant. That's why we work so hard to make sure that nobody ever gets disappointed by our meatloaf. And like Darlene, we start out by chopping up the best meat we can lay our hands on. There are not many things Threadgill's serves that are better than Mother used to make. One of them is meat-

Ordering meatloaf, like ordering a chopped beef sandwich, is the ultimate sign of trust in a restaurant.

loaf. Momma made meatloaf with hamburger meat. The kids in the nursery school loved it, but I hated it. It was too much like having a dry hamburger without the trimmings and with yucky stuff like celery inside. I didn't know the term back then, but I didn't like the "mouth feel."

I would respectfully ask to be allowed to make my meatloaf into a sandwich so I could slather it with mustard. It didn't hurt her feelings too much. After all, at the nursery school, meatloaf was just a dish made to accomplish a job, a utility meal, much like the cafe and diner lunches eaten by workers away from home.

I don't know where or when our modern American version of meatloaf was invented, but it might well have been in a cafe or diner where they needed to cook and hold hot meals in large numbers. The meals needed to be inexpensive and filling; they needed to be value meals.

Nowadays, Threadgill's has several entrées that fit the value-meal category. Some are easy-to-cook and easy-to-hold items like meatloaf or pork roast and some are made-to-order nightmares like chicken-fried steak.

There aren't any veal roasts or crown racks of lamb on Threadgill's menu, and there aren't any such recipes in this chapter. Threadgill's entrées are designed to anchor the meat and three and to be the centerpiece of old-fashioned value meals.

Fry It in the Skillet or Grill It

Chicken-Fried Steak
(or Pork Chop or Chicken Breast)
and Cream Gravy

8 6-ounce tenderized beef cutlets at room temperature (or tenderized center cut boneless pork chop, or tenderized boneless chicken breasts)
2 eggs
2 cups milk at room temperature
3 cups flour
2 teaspoons Meat Seasoning (see recipe, page 38)
2 cups *frying* oil, preferably canola
Skillet Cream Gravy (see recipe, page 52)

WHISK EGGS and milk together in a bowl and set this egg wash aside. Combine the flour and meat seasoning in another bowl and set aside. Heat the oil in a heavy 14-inch cast-iron skillet over medium heat to 350°. Use a 550° thermometer to check temperature. The oil should pop loudly when a drop of egg wash is dropped in. Dip each of the first 4 cutlets in the egg wash mixture. Dredge them in the flour, then dip them back into the egg wash, and very gently place them in the hot oil. As you carry them one at a time from the egg wash to the skillet, hold a plate under them to catch the dripping egg wash. There'll be a regular explosion of noisy oil a-popping. Cook for 3 to 5 minutes, until breading is set and golden brown. Gently turn them with a long-handled meat fork or long metal tongs. Be careful. Cook another 3 minutes. Carefully remove them from the skillet and drain on a platter lined with paper towels. Let oil reheat and repeat process for other 4 cutlets. Serve with Cream Gravy and Mashed Potatoes. **Makes 8 servings**.

☛ This wet-dry-wet method is the Threadgill's secret for sealing in the juices.

FRIED CHICKEN

1 cut-up fryer, 3½ pounds
Salt
Pepper
2 cups buttermilk
2 cups vegetable or peanut oil
2 cups flour

WASH THE CHICKEN and pat dry; sprinkle with salt and pepper. Soak in buttermilk as long as convenient, at least an hour. Heat oil in deep cast-iron frying pan to about 350°. Dip pieces into flour to coat thoroughly. Ease chicken into skillet (if frying more than one chicken, do the large pieces first, then hold them in a slightly warm oven while frying the smaller pieces. This will keep the fried pieces crisp). Cook about 6 to 8 minutes per side. For best results, do not use a lid on the skillet. Though a lid makes cleanup easier, it makes the crust too soggy. **Makes 4 to 6 servings,** depending on how you cut up the chicken.

☛ One Fried Chicken. (There is hardly ever a fit reason to fry just one chicken.)

FRIED CATFISH

8 catfish filets, 7 to 9 ounces each
2 eggs
2½ cups milk
1½ cups flour
1½ cups coarsely ground corn meal
3 tablespoons Seafood Seasoning (see recipe, page 39)
2½ cups *frying* oil, preferably canola

WHISK EGGS and milk together in a bowl and set this egg wash aside. Mix the flour, corn meal, and seasoning together in a bowl. Heat the oil in a 12-inch heavy cast-iron skillet over medium heat to 325°. Use a 550° thermometer to check temperature. The oil should pop loudly when a drop of egg wash is dropped in. Dip 4 of the filets in the egg wash mixture. Dredge them in the flour/meal mixture and then dip them back into the egg wash and very gently place them in the hot oil. As you carry them one at a time from the egg wash to the skillet, hold a plate under them to catch the dripping egg wash. There'll be a regular explosion of noisy oil a-popping. Cook for 3 to 5 minutes until breading is set and golden brown. Gently turn them with a pair of metal tongs. Be careful. Cook another 3 minutes. Carefully remove them from the skillet and drain on a platter lined with paper towels. Let oil return to temperature and repeat process for other filets. Serve with tartar and cocktail sauce. **Makes 8 servings.**

FRIED OYSTERS

4 pounds shucked oysters
2 cups flour
2 cups masa harina (specialty cornmeal)
2½ cups *frying* oil, preferably canola

MIX THE FLOUR and masa harina together in a bowl. Heat the oil in a 12-inch heavy cast-iron skillet over medium heat to 325°. Use a 550° thermometer to check temperature. Dredge half of the oysters in the flour mix and very gently place them in the hot oil. Cook for 4 to 6 minutes until breading is set and color is light golden brown. Keep the oysters from cooking together by separating with metal tongs. Be careful with the hot oil. Carefully remove oysters from the skillet and drain on a platter lined with paper towels. Let oil return to temperature and repeat process for rest of oysters. Serve with tartar and cocktail sauce. **Makes 8 servings.**

CATFISH MOUTARDE

8 catfish filets, 7 to 9 ounces each
2 eggs
2 cups milk
2 cups cooking oil
2 cups flour

BATTER:

1 cup Creole mustard
1 cup sour cream
$^1/_2$ cup milk
$^1/_2$ cup heavy cream
1 egg
1 tablespoon Worcestershire sauce
1 teaspoon Seafood Seasoning (see recipe, page 39)

WHISK 2 eggs and 2 cups milk together in a bowl and set this egg wash aside. Combine all the batter ingredients and whip well. This batter must be very smooth. Heat the oil in a 14-inch heavy cast-iron skillet over medium heat to 350°. Use a 550° thermometer to check temperature. The oil should pop loudly when a drop of egg wash is dropped in. Dip 4 of the filets in egg wash, then flour, then batter. Very gently place them in the hot oil. As you carry them one at a time to the skillet, hold a plate under them to catch the dripping egg wash. Cook for 4 to 5 minutes, until golden, and gently turn them with a pair of metal tongs. Be careful with the hot oil. Cook another 4 minutes. Carefully remove them from the skillet and drain on a platter lined with paper towels. Let oil return to temperature and repeat process for other filets. **Makes 8 servings.**

GRILLADES AND GRITS

5-pound boneless pork loin, cut into 1-inch squares, $^1/_2$-inch thick
2 tablespoons lard
3 tablespoons flour
2 small onions, chopped
1 large green bell pepper, chopped
2 cloves garlic, chopped
3 tomatoes, chopped
5 cups water or Chicken Stock (see recipe, page 34)
2 bay leaves
4 to 5 sprigs parsley, chopped
$^1/_2$ teaspoon salt
1 teaspoon pepper
1 quart cooked white grits, white rice, or mashed potatoes

BROWN the pork pieces in the lard. Remove from skillet and set aside. Add flour, onion, bell pepper, and garlic to fat in pan and brown thoroughly to make a roux. Add the tomatoes, stock, bay leaves, parsley, salt, and pepper. Bring to a boil and reduce to simmer. Simmer mixture about half an hour and then return the pork to the skillet. Simmer until the pieces will cut with a fork. Serve over grits, rice, or mashed potatoes. **Makes 8 servings.**

☛ These pork grillades were invented to avoid the expense of veal and the length of time it takes to cook beef to the right tenderness. They are a celebration of the new, improved pork. This is another example of my favorite things that frequently are the hardest to sell. First, this has been a traditional brunch item as served in southern Louisiana. Threadgill's is hardly a brunch kinda place. Second, folks around here don't eat things they've never heard of unless they're building their self-esteem by squandering a foolish amount of money with a waiter wearing a tuxedo shirt who pours on layers of delicious adjectives. Third, it's hard to sell pork these days. Fourth, it's even harder to sell grits.

What we try to do is sell it as a "Creole Holiday Dish" that's made up of "extra lean & tender pork" in a "spicy tomato gravy, served" (quickly now) "over grits, rice or mashed potatoes."

PORK STROGANOFF

2 pounds pork tenderloin, trimmed and cut into thin strips
3 tablespoons safflower oil
2 large onions, quartered and thinly sliced
14 ounces small button mushrooms, sliced
4 tablespoons whole wheat flour
$2\frac{1}{2}$ cups unsalted Chicken Stock (see recipe, page 34)
2 tablespoons tomato paste
2 teaspoons fresh lemon juice
$\frac{1}{2}$ teaspoon salt
Coarsely ground black pepper
$\frac{1}{2}$ cup plain low-fat yogurt
Cooked spinach fettucine, grits, white rice, or mashed potatoes

HEAT THE OIL in a large frying pan over medium-high heat until it is hot, not smoking. Add the pork strips and onion, and cook, stirring frequently, until the pork is browned all over, about 3 minutes. Stir in the mushrooms and cook for a minute more, stirring. Add the flour to the pan and mix well, then slowly stir in the stock and bring to a boil while stirring. Lower the heat and simmer for 2 minutes, then stir in the tomato paste, lemon juice, salt, and pepper. Heat the mixture over low heat for 2 minutes. Remove the pan from the heat, stir in the yogurt, and serve immediately over spinach fettuccine, grits, rice, or mashed potatoes. **Makes 8 to 10 servings.**

☛ If I ever try to sell this in the restaurant, it'll be during the South by Southwest Music Conference and we'll have to call it Nashville Stroganoff.

TENDERLOIN JAMBALAYA

2-pound pork tenderloin, rimmed and cubed
4 tablespoons safflower oil
2 onions, chopped
2 large garlic cloves, finely chopped
2 pounds ripe tomatoes, peeled and chopped, or canned whole tomatoes, chopped
4 cups pureed tomatoes
1 tablespoon chili powder
1 tablespoon Worcestershire sauce
Cayenne pepper
1 tablespoon salt
Coarse black pepper
Tabasco Sauce
1 green and 1 red bell pepper, seeded, deribbed, and diced
4 ribs celery, diced
1 eggplant, cubed
2 medium zucchini, cubed
2½ cups long-grain raw rice

HEAT 1 TABLESPOON of the oil in a large skillet over high heat. Add the pork cubes and cook for 2 minutes, stirring all the time. Stir in the onion and garlic, and cook for 2 minutes more. Add the chopped tomatoes, pureed tomatoes, chili powder, Worcestershire sauce, a pinch of cayenne pepper, salt, some coarsely ground black pepper, and a few drops of Tabasco Sauce. Stir well. Cover and cook over low heat for 25 minutes, stirring occasionally. Meanwhile, heat the remaining safflower oil in a frying pan over medium heat. Add the bell peppers, celery, and eggplant. Cook over low heat for 5 minutes, then stir in the zucchini and cook for another 5 minutes. Add the vegetables and rice to the meat mixture in the skillet, and stir to combine them. Cover and continue cooking until the rice is tender and all the excess liquid has been absorbed, about 15 minutes, maybe 20. (Depending on how much liquid the vegetables produce, you may need to add a bit of water from time to time.) Fluff up the rice and serve hot. **Makes 8 servings.**

Pastalaya

A marriage of lots of the ingredients traditional to Jambalaya with pasta instead of rice. Three great ways to eat huge portions of stuff that's really good for you. Just add a green salad.

Seafood Pastalaya

8 ounces shrimp, cut into 16 pieces
8 1-ounce pieces red snapper
8 ounces shucked oysters
$1\frac{1}{2}$ pounds fresh or frozen linguini, uncooked
$\frac{1}{8}$ cup olive oil
1 tablespoon Seafood Seasoning (see recipe, page 39)
1 green bell pepper, sliced
1 teaspoon garlic, minced
2 cups Chablis
3 cups Pastalaya Base (see recipe, page 48)
Parmesan cheese, shredded, or minced parsley for garnish
Black pepper

THAW LINGUINI if frozen. Heat enough water to cook linguini. When water boils, add linguini.

IN A 14-INCH skillet heat olive oil. Dust shrimp pieces with seafood seasoning. Sauté shrimp with bell pepper, turning so all sides cook evenly. Add the red snapper and garlic, then add oysters. Add wine and bring to a boil. Add Pastalaya Base and return to a boil. Reduce heat to low.

REMOVE LINGUINI when done and toss with sauce. Garnish with shredded parmesan cheese or parsley. Serve with black pepper. **Makes 4 large servings.**

CHICKEN PASTALAYA

2 pounds boneless, skinless chicken breasts, cut into 1-ounce pieces (about 32 squares)
1½ pounds linguini, uncooked
⅛ cup olive oil
1 tablespoon Poultry Seasoning (see recipe, page 38)
1 green bell pepper, sliced
1 clove garlic, minced
⅛ cup Chablis
2 cups Chicken Stock (see recipe, page 34)
3 cups Pastalaya Base (see recipe, page 48)
Parmesan cheese, shredded, or parsley for garnish
Black pepper

HEAT ENOUGH WATER to cook linguini. When it is boiling, add linguini.

IN A 14-INCH skillet heat olive oil. Dust chicken with poultry season-ing and sauté, turning so all sides cook evenly. Add bell pepper, then garlic and wine. Add chicken stock and bring to a boil. Add Pastalaya Base and bring back to a boil. Reduce heat to low.

DRAIN LINGUINI when done and toss with sauce. Garnish with shred-ded parmesan cheese or parsley. Serve with black pepper. **Makes 4 servings.**

VEGETABLE PASTALAYA

1½ pounds spinach fettucine, fresh or frozen, uncooked
¼ cup olive oil, scant
1 green bell pepper, sliced
1 carrot, julienned
1 stalk broccoli flowerets, cut
1 yellow squash, core trimmed, julienned
1 clove garlic, minced
½ pound mushrooms, sliced

1 tablespoon Vegetable Seasoning (see recipe, page 39)
$^1/_8$ cup Chablis
2 cups Vegetable Stock (see recipe, page 36)
3 cups Pastalaya Base (see recipe, page 48)
Parmesan cheese, shredded, or minced parsley for garnish
Black pepper

THAW FETTUCINE if frozen. Heat enough water to cook fettucine (linguini may be used as a substitute). When water boils, add fettucine.

IN A 12-INCH nonstick skillet, heat olive oil. Sauté bell pepper and carrot, stirring or tossing. Add broccoli, squash, garlic, and vegetable seasoning. Continue stirring. Add mushrooms and stir. Add Chablis and stock. Bring to a boil. Add Pastalaya Base and return to a boil. Reduce heat to low.

REMOVE FETTUCINE when done and toss with sauce. Garnish with shredded parmesan cheese or minced parsley. Serve with black pepper. **Makes 4 large servings.**

☛ One of the reasons our vegetarians love Threadgill's so.

BEEF LIVER WITH ONIONS

8 4-ounce beef livers, sliced, not frozen
1 cup vegetable oil
1 cup flour
2 tablespoons Meat Seasoning (see recipe, page 38)
2 quarts yellow onion, thinly sliced
2 cups Brown Gravy (see recipe, page 53)

HEAT half the oil in a 12-inch skillet over medium heat. Add seasoning to flour. Dredge livers in flour and gently place in hot oil. Cook about 3 minutes or until meat is medium brown. Turn carefully using a meat fork or metal tongs. When livers are cooked through, remove to heated dish, add rest of oil to skillet, and cook onions until soft. Serve onions on top of livers with brown gravy. **Makes 8 servings.**

☛ I remember hearing Mother advise the young pregnant mothers who already had kids in the nursery school, "Eat some liver. You've gotta get your iron." There are two secrets to perfect liver: Don't overcook it, and use good brown gravy.

Bronzed Catfish, Chicken Breast or Sirloin Steak

8 8-ounce entrées—
catfish filets,
boneless chicken breasts,
or sirloin steaks

$\frac{1}{2}$ pound (2 sticks) butter, melted
4 tablespoons Seasoning (Seafood or Poultry or Meat) (see recipes, pages 38–39)

PREHEAT a dry 14-inch cast-iron skillet to 400°. (A grill thermometer will measure the temperature.) Dredge 4 of the entrées in the melted butter and evenly coat both sides with seasoning. Carefully place entrées in hot skillet and cook about 3 to 4 minutes on each side. Steak will be medium-rare. Use same process for other 4 entrées. The catfish is also excellent served over our Spinach Casserole as a Florentine dish. **Makes 8 servings.**

NOTE: The chicken and steak can be sliced for excellent additions to many salads.

SOUTHWEST PORK CHOPS

8 6-ounce boneless pork chops

2 cups Smoked Corn Relish (see recipe, page 50)
$^{3}/_{4}$ cup Chipotle Cream Sauce (see recipe, page 47)

GRILL THE CHOPS until done, about 4 minutes on each side. On each chop place ¼ cup relish and 1½ tablespoons Chipotle Sauce. **Makes 8 servings.**

NOTE: This technique is also fine for boneless chicken breasts and many fish and steaks.

SMOKED CHICKEN PASTA SALAD

4 pounds smoked chicken meat
$^{1}/_{2}$ cup Vinegar and Oil Dressing (see recipe, page 44)
1 recipe French Quarter Pasta Salad (see recipe, page 67)

1 head leaf lettuce
1 pound cherry tomatoes
1 red onion, thinly sliced
Parmesan cheese and black pepper for garnish

DICE THE CHICKEN into bite-sized pieces, and toss with about half the dressing. Place pasta salad over green leaf lettuce on 8 chilled plates and top with chicken. Garnish with cherry tomatoes and thinly sliced rings of red onion. Moisten with remainder of Vinegar and Oil Dressing. Serve shredded parmesan cheese and black pepper on the side. **Makes 8 salads.**

Bronzed Sirloin Pasta Salad

4 8-ounce bronzed sirloin steaks (see recipe, page 127)
$^1/_3$ cup Vinegar and Oil Dressing (see recipe, page 44)
1 head leaf lettuce
1 recipe French Quarter Pasta Salad (see recipe, page 67)
1 pound cherry tomatoes
1 red onion, thinly sliced
Parmesan cheese and black pepper for garnish

Bronze steaks as in recipe, chill. Very thinly slice the meat across the grain, trimming excess fat, if any. Toss with about half the dressing. On 8 chilled plates lay a bed of leaf lettuce, then pasta salad, and then sliced steak. Garnish with cherry tomatoes and sliced red onion. Moisten with remaining dressing. Serve shredded parmesan and black pepper on the side. **Makes 8 salads.**

Note: Substitute smoked tomatoes for cherry tomatoes for a real taste treat.

Oven Foods

Meatloaf

4 pounds ground chuck
1 cup medium yellow onion, chopped
1 cup celery, chopped
1 green bell pepper, chopped
2 cups bread crumbs
3 eggs, beaten
1/2 cup cream or milk
1 tablespoon steak sauce
1 teaspoon black pepper
1/2 teaspoon salt
4 thick slices bacon (optional)
Creole Sauce **(see recipe, page 46)**

PREHEAT OVEN to 350°. Mix all ingredients except bacon by hand until well blended. Divide in half and shape into 2 loaves about 8x4x3 inches. Place 2 thick slices of bacon on top of each loaf, if desired, and bake on greased rack of roasting pan for 75 minutes. Meanwhile, prepare Creole Sauce. Slice thick or thin and top with a generous amount of Creole Sauce. **Makes 8 to 12 servings.**

☛ Oh, succulent pâté of the plains! I just cannot even begin to describe the delicious pleasure of Threadgill's blue plate meatloaf with Creole Sauce and deep, rich, fragrant brown gravy over soft, hot buttery mashed potatoes. At $4.95, plus a glass of iced tea and a small salad, I'll challenge any restaurant meal in America to a taste bud-to-taste bud, dollar-to-dollar comparison. Throw in desserts and I'll double the bet. I think our meatloaf could appear on plates in the most expensive restaurants in America and receive raves for the chef.

GLAZED HAM WITH JEZEBEL SAUCE

10-pound ham at room temperature
Pineapple rings
Whole cloves
Jezebel Sauce (see recipe, page 48)

PREHEAT OVEN to 375°. Baste the ham with Jezebel Sauce. Wrap loosely in foil. Place in a roasting pan. Bake at 375° for 2½ hours. Remove from foil and trim fat. Score with 2-inch, X-patterned "shrapnel cut," ¾ inch deep. Insert ¼-inch thick pineapple rings into cuts, secure with cloves. Bake another hour at 400°, basting again after 30 minutes. Slice into ½-inch thick steaks. Serve with Jezebel Sauce on the side. **Makes about 10 servings.**

NASHVILLE MEATLOAF

4 cups ground ham
4 cups lean ground pork
2 eggs, lightly beaten
2 onions, finely chopped
1 green bell pepper, finely chopped
1 teaspoon dried chervil
1 teaspoon dried rosemary
Freshly ground pepper
2 cups milk
1½ cups brown sugar
1 teaspoon dry mustard
½ cup cider vinegar
6 slices fresh pineapple
2 tablespoons red currant jelly

PREHEAT OVEN to 375°. Combine ham, pork, eggs, chopped onion and green pepper, chervil, rosemary, a few turns of the pepper grinder, and milk. Mix sugar, mustard, and vinegar and spread on bottom of a well-greased loaf pan. Trim pineapple slices, cutting out core, and press them into the sugar-mustard mixture in a large loaf pan. Fill holes with jelly. Fill pan with ham mixture. Bake for about 1½ hours. (If loaf browns too fast, reduce heat and cover top with greased paper.) **Makes about 8 servings.**

☛ In Tennesee folks have better sense about using pork than they do in some other parts of the country. When I was running the AWHQ, Charlie Daniels asked me if I'd ever had meatloaf made with pork instead of beef. I hadn't, but the idea sounded so good that I finally got around to experimenting with every pork substitution I could think of, from Chicken-Fried Pork Chop to this recipe. Charlie was on a diet so I didn't name it after him.

SMOTHERED PORK CHOPS

8 6-ounce boneless pork chops
12 tablespoons (1½ sticks) margarine
1 cup chopped celery
1 cup yellow onion, thinly sliced
1 cup flour
8 cups Chicken Stock (see recipe, page 34)
1 pound mushrooms, thinly sliced
1 teaspoon celery salt
1 teaspoon salt
1 teaspoon sage
2 tablespoons black pepper

PREHEAT OVEN to 350°. Melt margarine and brown the chops lightly on both sides. Set aside. Sauté celery and onions in margarine. Set aside. Add flour to pan to make roux and cook lightly. Add stock and stir until thickened into gravy. Add mushrooms and seasonings. Put vegetables in baking pan and put chops on top. Smother with gravy and bake in a covered dish at 350° for about 45 minutes. **Makes 4 servings.**

French Quarter Catfish

8 catfish filets, 7 to 9 ounces each

Marinade:

1 cup Chablis
1 teaspoon thyme
2 tablespoons cider vinegar
2 bay leaves
1/4 cup vegetable oil
1/2 teaspoon cayenne pepper
1/2 teaspoon sugar
1/2 teaspoon dry mustard

Bread Crumb Topping:

6 tablespoons butter
1 teaspoon garlic, minced
4 cups bread crumbs
Lemon and parsley for garnish

Make marinade, mixing all ingredients well. Marinate filets for 4 hours, turning once. Preheat oven to 350°. Sauté garlic in butter and mix well with bread crumbs. Drain filets well and arrange on greased baking sheet. Cover catfish with crumb mixture. Bake in covered pan for 10 minutes and remove cover to brown crumbs. Cook about 10 more minutes or until flaky. Garnish with lemon and parsley. **Makes 8 servings.**

Seafood Jambalaya

Rice:

4 tablespoons margarine or butter
1/2 cup yellow onion, diced
1/2 cup green bell pepper, diced
1 green onion, chopped
4 cups fish stock or oyster liquor
1/2 teaspoon turmeric
2 cups converted long-grain rice

JAMBALAYA BASE:

4 tablespoons butter or margarine
4 cups yellow onion, diced
1 cup celery, diced
2 green bell peppers, diced
2 jalapeños, minced
1 tablespoon garlic, minced
1 cup cauliflower, chopped
2½ pounds tomatoes, diced
1 cup cherry tomatoes, halved
2 cups tomato sauce
1 pound shrimp, peeled, deveined, and diced
1 pound shucked oysters, sliced
1 teaspoon Tabasco Sauce
¼ cup picante sauce, medium
1 tablespoon Seafood Seasoning (see recipe, page 39)
Green onions for garnish

RICE: Preheat oven to 350°. Melt margarine and sauté onion and bell pepper. Place all ingredients in covered casserole dish and bake in oven until rice is just done, about 25 minutes.

BASE: In heavy 14-inch skillet, melt margarine and sauté onion. Add celery, bell pepper, jalapeño, and garlic, stirring to cook evenly. Add cauliflower and stir again. Add all other ingredients and bring to a boil, stirring. Reduce heat to simmer and cook about 20 minutes.

MIX BASE with rice, garnish with green onions, and serve. **Makes 10 servings.**

SPINACH AND OYSTER PIE

4 tablespoons butter or margarine
1½ cups Italian bread crumbs
½ cup parmesan cheese
2 cups Spinach Casserole (see recipe, page 110)
1 pint shucked oysters

PREHEAT OVEN to 350°. Melt the butter and pour into 8x11-inch pan. In a separate bowl, combine the crumbs and cheese. Pour ¾ of the crumb and cheese mixture into the butter, forming a shell in the bottom of the pan. Fill with Spinach Casserole and cover with oysters. Top with the rest of the crumbs. Bake for 20 minutes, then broil to brown (about 2 minutes). **Makes 4 servings.**

STUFFED TROUT

8 trout, headless and deboned (8 ounces average)
6 tablespoons butter
¾ cup yellow onion, diced
¾ cup celery, diced
2 tablespoons garlic, minced
1 tablespoon jalapeño, minced
¼ cup flour
¼ cup green onion, diced
1 tablespoon Seafood Seasoning (see recipe, page 39)
½ pound crabmeat, picked
¾ cup fish stock
1 tablespoon Creole mustard
3 tablespoons red bell pepper, diced
1 tablespoon parsley, minced
¾ cup bread crumbs
Lemon wedges and parsley for garnish

PREHEAT OVEN to 350°. Wash trout well. Caramelize onion in butter. Add celery, garlic, and jalapeño. Add flour. Cook 3 to 4 minutes. Add green onions and Seafood Seasoning. Add crab, stock, mustard, red bell peppers, and parsley. Add bread crumbs as needed for desired consistency. Stuff trout and bake in 350° oven for about 25 minutes. Brown under broiler if desired. Garnish with parsley and lemon wedges. **Makes 8 servings.**

SPINACH PIZZA

2 large Boboli pizza shells
$^1/_3$ cup olive oil
2 cloves garlic, minced
Anchovy paste (optional)
2 tablespoons Prudhomme's Pizza & Pasta Seasoning
2 cups Spinach Casserole (see recipe, page 110)
10 ounces mozzarella cheese, shredded

PREHEAT OVEN to 450°. Add the minced garlic to the olive oil and brush evenly over both pizza shells. Dot with anchovy paste if desired. Sprinkle with Pizza & Pasta Seasoning. Spread half the Spinach Casserole over each shell. Top with cheese and bake 8 to 10 minutes or until cheese bubbles and shells are crispy. **Makes 6 servings.**

CHICKEN ENCHILADAS

5 pounds chicken thigh meat, boiled and chopped
$^3/_4$ cup green bell pepper, chopped
$1^1/_2$ cups celery
$1^1/_2$ cups yellow onion, chopped
$2^1/_2$ cups tomato sauce
1 teaspoon black pepper
1 teaspoon salt
1 teaspoon cumin
$2^1/_2$ tablespoons Poultry Seasoning (see recipe, page 38)
16 corn tortillas
1 pound Monterrey Jack cheese, grated
1 quart Salsa Verde (see recipe, page 137)
Sour cream

TO MAKE FILLING: Put all ingredients except tortillas, cheese, Salsa Verde, and sour cream in stock pot and bring to a boil. Reduce to a simmer and cook for 45 minutes.

TO ASSEMBLE ENCHILADAS: Preheat oven to 350°. Soften tortillas in hot oil or over boiling water. Roll meat sauce into tortilla to create enchiladas. Place enchiladas in an oiled baking pan. Sprinkle cheese over each enchilada, cover pan, and bake until cheese melts, about 10 minutes. Serve enchiladas with Salsa Verde and sour cream. **Makes 8 servings (16 enchiladas).**

SALSA VERDE

2 pounds tomatillos, peeled, boiled, and chopped
1 teaspoon jalapeño, chopped
1 tablespoon cilantro, chopped
1/4 cup yellow onion, minced
1 teaspoon salt

COMBINE ALL INGREDIENTS in a small stock pot. Bring to a boil, then reduce heat and simmer 30 minutes. **Makes 1 quart.**

POT FOODS

There was something about pot food that said "there may be some company coming." Around our house pot food and cold weather seemed to go together, but on trips to visit folks in Louisiana and Mississippi, weather didn't seem to matter much. From gumbo to chili, their pots were always big and we were always welcome. "How'd they know we were coming, Momma?" "They didn't know, sugar. They just always eat this way."

Dipping and sopping seemed to be the only differences between some appetizers and entrées. Chips and crackers or cornbread were the clues as to whether or not something else was to follow.

CHICKEN AND DUMPLINGS

CHICKEN:

2 whole chickens, 2½–3 pounds each
2 bay leaves
1 teaspoon tarragon
1 teaspoon thyme
12 peppercorns
2 cloves garlic
1 cup yellow onion, diced
1 cup carrots, sliced ½-inch thick
1 rib celery, cut in 2-inch slices
½ cup flour
1 teaspoon Tabasco Sauce
1 teaspoon black pepper
1 teaspoon salt

DUMPLINGS:

3 cups Biscuit Mix (see recipe, page 76)
1 cup milk

PUT CHICKENS in a stock pot with bay leaves, tarragon, thyme, peppercorns, and garlic, cover with cold water, and bring to a boil. Reduce heat and simmer about 30 minutes or until chicken is just short of done. Wash and prepare vegetables, putting trimmings into stock pot. Carefully remove chickens from pot, leaving stock at a simmer. Let chickens cool slightly and remove meat from the birds, putting bones and skins back into stock pot. Check meat again carefully for bones. You should have almost 2 pounds of chicken meat.

MIX BISCUIT MIX with milk. On lightly floured surface, roll out dough ⅜-inch thick. Cut into ½-inch squares and set aside. Strain stock and reserve fat from top. Use flour and enough fat to make a light roux. In large pot, put vegetables and 1 gallon of stock. Bring to a boil, add dumplings and 6 tablespoons of roux. Reduce to a simmer, stirring to keep dumplings from sticking. Add chicken meat, Tabasco, black pepper, and salt. Cook until dumplings are done, about 20 minutes. **Makes 8 to 10 servings.**

BEEF STEW

3 pounds stew meat
2 ounces vegetable oil
2 cloves garlic, finely chopped
2 cups tomatoes, diced
1 bay leaf
8 cups Beef Stock (see recipe, page 34)
1/2 cup celery, chopped
1 cup yellow onion, chopped
1/2 pound carrots, sliced 1/2-inch thick
1 pound potatoes, diced same size as beef
1 teaspoon black pepper
1 cup green peas
1 teaspoon chopped parsley
1/4 cup flour
Salt to taste

BROWN stew meat in oil. Add garlic, tomatoes, bay leaf, and stock. Bring to a boil, reduce heat, and simmer for 1 hour or until meat is tender. Add celery, onion, carrots, potatoes, and black pepper. Simmer for 1 more hour. Add peas and parsley. Make a paste with the flour and a little water. Blend paste until smooth with a wire whip and stir into stew. Simmer until slightly thickened. Salt to taste and correct the seasonings. **Makes 10 servings.**

Dark brown flavor through and through,
sometimes nothing else will do.
I eat it at night, eat it in the morning,
eat it till I'm bent over. Groaning.
(My apologies to Guy Clark and Roy Blount, Jr.)

POT ROAST

5-pound chuck roast
1/4 cup vegetable oil
2 cups tomatoes, diced
4 stalks celery, cut in 1-inch chunks
2 carrots, cut in 1-inch chunks

1 large potato, cut in 1-inch chunks
2 cloves garlic, whole
1 cup yellow onion, sliced
$^1/_2$ teaspoon salt
1 teaspoon black pepper
1 bay leaf
5 cups Beef Stock (see recipe, page 34)

PREHEAT OVEN to 350°. Trim excess fat from roast. In a large skillet, use oil to brown roast on all sides. Transfer roast to 2-gallon roasting pan, sauté vegetables in skillet, and add everything to roasting pan. Cover and place in 400° oven. After 1 hour, remove from oven and turn meat over. Cover and return to oven for about 1 more hour or until center of meat reaches a temperature of 160°. Remove from oven and cut meat into 2-ounce chunks to serve. Remove vegetables with slotted spoon and serve with meat. **Makes 8 servings.**

☛ Similar song, similar verse, this is a combination pot and oven dish. I am especially crazy about the roasted potatoes in this recipe.

TEXAS RED CHILI

$^1/_2$ pound (2 sticks) margarine, melted
8 cups onion, chopped
2 cups green bell pepper, chopped
2 cups celery, chopped
4 jalapeños, minced
1 tablespoon garlic, minced
1 tablespoon Meat Seasoning (see recipe, page 38)
3 ounces chili mix (Two-Alarm is fine)
$2^1/_2$ pounds chili meat
1 cup Beef Stock (see recipe, page 34)
2 quarts tomatoes, diced
Salt to taste

IN A 2-GALLON POT melt the margarine and cook the onions, bell peppers, and celery until the onions are transparent. Add the jalapeños, garlic, Meat Seasoning, and chili mix and cook for 10 minutes. Add chili meat, stock, and diced tomatoes and simmer until all of the flavors are balanced, 1 to 2 hours. Add salt to taste. **Makes 10 servings.**

☛ One of the great advantages of a giant pot of homemade chili is that it freezes really well. Another is that, unlike many pot foods, chili is nearly perfect as soon as it has finished cooking. Sure, it is perfect the next day, but around here even the most bitter of cold fronts (a blue norther) is frequently gone by the next day and, just as frequently, the next day finds me having had enough chili until the next blue norther. If the cold front lasts, there's hardly a better Texas breakfast than chili over toast topped with a fried egg.

MUMBO-GUMBO

ROUX:

4 tablespoons vegetable oil
7 tablespoons flour

GUMBO:

1 cup okra, sliced thick
1 cup tomatoes, peeled
2 quarts fish stock or Chicken Stock (see recipe, page 34)
1 teaspoon Seafood Seasoning (see recipe, page 39)
½ pound headless shrimp, peeled and deveined
½ pound cooked andouille or smoked sausage, sliced
½ pound cooked ham, diced
½ pound cooked turkey or chicken, diced
½ cup Creole Sauce (see recipe, page 46)
1 teaspoon cayenne pepper
½ teaspoon salt
4 cups Vegetarian Jambalaya (see recipe, page 112)

COOK ROUX to a medium dark, and cool. Heat okra and tomato in a 4-quart pot. As they heat, crush completely. Add stock and boil. Add seasoning and meats and return to boil. Add Creole Sauce and roux and mix well. Allow to simmer 20 minutes. Add cayenne pepper and salt to taste. Serve 1 cup over ½ cup Jambalaya. **Makes 8 servings.**

RARE STEAKS

It may strike some as odd that beef played a relatively minor role in our Southern comfort food format. Texas, oil wells, cattle drives and big steaks seem to be married in the minds of most Americans. If you care to share a common practice among Southern Depression-era cooks like my mom or old restaurant operators like me, keep track of the cost per serving of the recipes in this collection. You'll quickly realize why Mother was always a bit scared of beef. It could surely wallop a budget out of whack and led to adventures involving a chest freezer in the garage and purchases of huge half and whole cows, sorted and wrapped by cut. It also led to more ground beef in the diet than I cared for. Beulah whaled away with her meat hammer at cheap cuts of meat, hoping the broiler and a lump of butter would render up a chewable steak. Woody had to replace her hammer's wooden handle with one made of pipe. The serving of any beef other than hamburgers, meatloaf, pot roast, chicken-fried steaks or veal cutlets was a rarity until my teenage years. The combination of Mother's successful nursery school and Dad's increasing plumber's wages began to make our lives feel pretty secure. Maybe that's why I think of this section as Rare Steaks. We didn't have them often then, and even today I have them less than I wish, though for other reasons. When I do eat steak, I want a rare steak of rare quality.

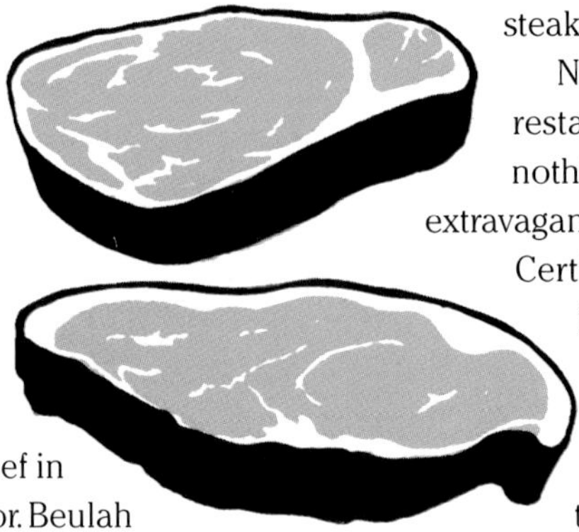

Nowadays at the restaurant we use nothing but the most extravagant beef I can buy. Certified Angus Beef is a marketing effort I endorse 100%. It is my way of ensuring that I've got carefully picked, aged beef of the highest possible quality money can buy. Using only whole muscle, ground chuck and the finest cuts of steak, I am always confident that when customers decide to splurge at Threadgill's on a big T-bone or filet of sirloin, they will be as satisfied as those who order a chicken-fried steak or the unbelievable meatloaf. CAB is available in only a few grocery stores around the country and is worth asking for.

My relationship with my meat purveyor over the last 15 years has developed into one of those storybook tales that make being in the food business a joy.

Rare-Medium Rare

When you cook steaks at home you can improve a rare steak easily by removing it from the fridge long enough ahead of time for it to reach room temperature. If you take steaks straight from a fridge to the skillet or grill, they are too cold in the middle.

The steak house may have been the first uniquely American "upscale" restaurant format.There is one version that is over a hundred years old. Lots of famous places have served it with very little variation and I recognize it as a nearly perfect way to celebrate. First a shrimp cocktail. Then the largest, finest, rarest steak that will fit on a platter, with just enough room left over for a serving of creamed spinach and a pile of fried potatoes. Cheesecake for dessert.

Pork

Pork is probably the most historically important meat in Southern cooking. A pig has so much useful meat that it became a major form of currency from before the Civil War through the Depression. Smoked, salted, ground into sausage, packed in lard, it was a major source of protein but it caused a lot of illness and carried a dangerous reputation. It is perhaps the most improved food item of this century. Over the last 30 years the safe cooking temperature of pork has dropped 10 degrees each decade. It is no longer necessary to cook over 150 degrees. The notion that slightly pink pork is perfectly okay will take another 20 years to sell, but then it took tomatoes almost 200 years to be considered safe by everyone.

There is not an easier major meal to cook than a pork roast.Your butcher will give it to you boned and a good grocery has plenty to choose from in the way of rubs.

"The Other White Meat" has been a successful promotion recently, but it hasn't always been so. The Pig Stand drive-in was the most dramatic chain in America at one time but it was not because of its slogan, "Eat a Pig Sandwich." More hamburgers were sold under the sign of the pig than anything else.

Mrs. Curtis's 1,200-page *Cook Book* in 1914 begins with the line: "The main object of this book is economy." Indeed, the Southern farm format for putting food on the family table was geared to pork, chicken and garden vegetables because economy was the key to survival. The pantry lined with jars of preserved vegetables and the smokehouse filled with pork were the family food bank. The enormous amount of nutrition provided by pigs made them just about the most valuable source of protein for the table. It is a wonder that more people didn't die of food poisoning. Ground pork patties, cooked and stored in buckets of lard in the smokehouse, were dipped up and warmed on the home comfort range without so much as a casualty. It doesn't paint a very pretty picture except for those with memories of savory aromas and succulent meals.

HAM

It is hard to knock the New Age rage for spiral-cut ham unless you have seen some of the hams processed. They are dipped in thick sugar water and literally glazed with a blowtorch. Mother's Restaurant in New Orleans is the last bastion of perfect ham. They have not even given in to the commercial slicer, much less a spiral-cut saw. They bake an incredible number of hams every day and they slice them each by hand. They char the edges, trim the surface before slicing them and place the "black ham" in a pan for customers to nibble while waiting in line to order a meal. It is one of the tastiest treats in New Orleans and it is free!

SANDWICHES AND PICNICS

Central Texans have many advantages over the rest of the world simply because of the weather. In Austin, there is a way to judge the weather that tells a lot more about Austin than whether it is cold or hot or raining or not. We have a separate column for Glorious! days. They have the effect of producing more picnics per year than seem natural to our friends in the North. As I write this description we are iced in by the worst freeze in 10 years. "Froze Closed!" the sign would read if we didn't have so many staff who live in walking (or slipping and sliding) distance of the restaurant. Even so, there is good news for picnic season in this occasional hazard: Mother Nature is the best exterminator and this is the way she can best bless our spring and summer. "Please freeze the fleas and the chiggers and ticks, too. I know that praying about the fire ants is probably pushing what you're inclined to do."

The success of Threadgill's ever-growing menu has been made possible in no small measure because we have refused to serve hamburgers. It

was not easy to argue with the customers who plopped down and insisted, "Just gimme a burger." Somehow, perhaps because we are priced in a modest range and have a diner-looking attachment on one side of an old filling station, many first-time customers assume that we serve burgers and malts. Because they have to read the menu to find out what they are going to order, many of our customers have stumbled upon things they would never have ordered otherwise. There is no denying that American food reaches its zenith of flavor in a double-meat-and-cheese with bacon and mayo. All flavor comes from fat, and when you add the sweetness of a glass of soda water and a pile of fries with ketchup, there is little wonder that America is addicted to burgers.

◆

Sandwiches are about hand-to-mouth food architecture, textures and flavors in endless variety.

◆

After being open 365 days a year, year after year, it became apparent that Threadgill's needed a couple of classy burger substitutes just to keep the staff from going nuts. Besides, it is easier to offer a sandwich as a substitute. "How 'bout a B.L.T., a grilled cheese or a hot roast beef, with fries?"

Three true American classics that'd do any juke joint proud. They are grill-top sandwiches, better suited to eating at a table with plenty of napkins than in a car. The B.L.T. and the grilled cheese or ham and cheese share the same taste and tactile perfection that is unique to lightly buttered bread that is grilled to a light crispness. The hot roast beef sandwich is much more than a handful. It is a plateful. It is unique in that we roast to medium-rare a 10-pound inside round of beef, then chill it so that it will slice thin and pink. No leftovers here. But just as important is the husky brown gravy made from roasted bones. There's no way to discuss in polite company the wonders of grilled and buttered bread smothered under rare roast beef that's covered with brown gravy puddling into a pile of fried potatoes and ketchup.

Most of the things we serve as entrées make wonderful sandwiches. The chicken-fried steak, pork chop and chicken breast. The meatloaf, fried shrimp and oysters, migas, and sausage. They all just need the right combination of bread and "dressing," as they say in New Orleans. "You want that Poboy dressed?" The sandwich is worthy of a whole book. The combinations are nearly limitless. (I make a better sandwich than the world will ever know about because, with the exception of the three on the Threadgill's menu, I only make them one or two at a time. In the same way that I refuse to compete with the hamburger industry, I refuse to make sandwiches for anyone but Sandra and me.)

The best commercial sandwiches in the world are produced by hand in New Orleans at the intersection of Poydras and Tchoupitoulas in Mother's Restaurant. The only argument I will entertain about this statement is which of the sandwiches on Mother's menu is the best. The Ferdi Special has won most of the awards and usually gets my vote too, but there are times when the Fried Oyster and Shrimp Combo is a requirement. It was at Mother's that I learned to substitute slaw whenever possible for lettuce. The cabbage, even shredded into angel hair, will still be crisp long after lettuce is soggy and disgusting. I learned how to cut the Poboy loaf—almost, but not quite, in two—so that it will hold together till it is unwrapped and then tugged apart easily to divide in half to eat. It was also there that I discovered "debris" and black ham and learned to stay calm in the midst of chaos and hullabaloo. I learned to stand quietly in the crowd until time to stand out and order resolutely.

This book is not about Mother's—it is about Threadgill's. But I gotta give credit where it is due and this little piece about sandwiches wouldn't be complete if I didn't urge you to visit this fine establishment when you're traveling through New Orleans. The half hour you spend there getting your breakfast and a couple of sandwiches to go will be the most thorough dose of Naw'lins available in such a short span of time.

When I was a tyke I used to say that the first thing I learned to cook was a peanut butter sandwich. My aunts thought it was cute. Then I learned to fix hot dogs and I got the attention of an uncle. Next came the hamburgers, grilled cheese, B.L.T., and pimiento cheese sandwiches. (Pimiento cheese on white bread may or may not be popular in other parts of the country. I've got no way to know. I was told recently that the three biggest markets in the country for grocery store sales of pimiento cheese are Dallas, San Antonio and Houston.)

Sandwiches are about hand-to-mouth food architecture, textures and flavors in endless variety. It is a wonder that something so wonderful in the way of food would be named for a British politician but not so curious as if it were named for a British cook. Several bastardizations of a good thing—the bachelor habit of eating at the kitchen counter, standing up, and eating while driving—have eroded the reputation of sandwiches.

If you could add up the number of hamburgers and sandwiches served every day in America (not to mention other fast food like pizza and chicken) it would paint a pretty clear picture of the diminished role of the household kitchen. Even the dining room at home is losing its role to the automobile.

And speaking of the automobile: Picnics go hand in hand with the Southern romance with the automobile. Picnics are not necessarily about eating outside. They are about eating in out-of-the-way places, romantic spots, breaking the rules, doing something once, never to be repeated, trying to always be prepared and certainly always making do with what there is available. Springing a successful picnic on an unsuspecting loved one is as close as most of us'll ever get to being a great movie producer or poet or choreographer or Willie Nelson. I've had a marvelous meal under a bridge, just barely out of a driving rain.

◆

Springing a successful picnic on an unsuspecting loved one is as close as most of us'll ever get to being a great movie producer or poet or choreographer or Willie Nelson.

◆

Watermelon Dream
by Guy Clark

The Sun was hot, and the dust rose up like
smoke,
So we hid beneath the elm tree and watched
the watermelons float
There in a big ol' tub of ice
And we'd split 'em open with a kitchen knife
and everybody got a slice of Watermelon Dream

Chorus
Ain't nothin' sweeter than a Watermelon Dream
'Cept sittin' on the porch eatin' that
peach ice cream
When life is really sweeter than it seems
That's what you call a watermelon dream

With sticky hands and faces we fought the
yellow jackets to a draw
Then we used the rind for second base
and played a little hardball
I don't know how much we ate
But all got the belly ache
And everybody stayed up way too late
It was a Watermelon Dream

B.L.T.

4 slices bacon
2 slices whole wheat bread
3 thick slices ripe tomato
1 tablespoon mayonnaise
Leaf lettuce

COOK BACON and toast bread. Assemble sandwich, slice in half on the diagonal, and enjoy with some pickles.

☛ A Southern Baptist Reuben—not one for the car. We use apple-smoked bacon from Peterson's Natural Farms, Clifton, Texas.

GRILLED HAM AND CHEESE

2 slices white bread
2 1-ounce slices ham
2 thick slices ripe tomato
2 ounces cheddar cheese, grated

TOAST BREAD on one side. Grill ham and tomatoes. Turn bread over and place ham, tomatoes, and cheese on bread. When cheese is melted, put sandwich together and slice on the diagonal. Enjoy with a pickle.

VARIATION: Omit the ham for a perfect grilled cheese.

Hymn to Ham

by Roy Blount, Jr.

Ham's substantial, ham is fat,
Ham is firm and sound.
Ham's what God was getting at
When he made pigs so round.

HOT ROAST BEEF SANDWICH

1/4 pound roast beef (about 6 thin slices)
1 slice whole wheat bread
1/4 cup Brown Gravy (see recipe, page 53)

TOAST BREAD on both sides. Cover toast with half the brown gravy. Place hot roast beef on top and cover with rest of brown gravy. Perfect with mashed potatoes also covered with brown gravy.

☛ The right bread, lightly toasted or grilled, is the important first step. Toast made on a griddle is buttery and makes a sandwich that will cause you to leave fingerprints.

Why is it that most sandwiches made on square bread are much better when sliced diagonally? The pie-shaped points fit further into the taste buds without hanging up on the corners of your smile.

CHICKEN SALAD SANDWICH

4 pounds boneless chicken breasts
2 tablespoons Poultry Seasoning (see recipe, page 38)
16 slices whole wheat bread
3 cups celery, diced
1 cup red onion, diced
2 tablespoons parsley, minced
2 teaspoons garlic, minced
2 cups mayonnaise
2 tablespoons honey
2 tablespoons lemon juice
1 teaspoon ginger
1 tablespoon black pepper

SPRINKLE Poultry Seasoning on both sides of chicken and bake until fully cooked. Mix other ingredients. Dice chicken and mix. Refrigerate. Toast bread, assemble sandwich. Lettuce optional. **Makes 8 sandwiches.**

NOTE: This dish is greatly enhanced by smoking the chicken!

GRAND PRIZE BEER
COTTON SEED
CLABBER GIRL
BAKING POWDER

DESSERTS

This is the covered dish category that always had the most entries at our family reunion.

Home Economics classes in the public schools may have been the cause of the dessert explosion in America. The classes were short and they came at all times during the day. You couldn't walk the halls between classes swapping pot roast and mashed potatoes, but cookies of a million sorts surely did make easy gifts. Sugar and little girls were equally as sweet at Baker Junior High and I learned quickly that saying "thank you" made up for not being able to dunk a basketball.

Ben & Jerry are heroes of mine for lots of reasons. For one thing, they don't apologize for not being skinny. They seem to share my abhorrence for secrets. Their ice cream recipe book reveals everything you need to know about making ice cream and we have used it to invent our own flavors.

When Dreyer's Grand Ice Cream planned their move into Texas, they asked us to suggest some Threadgill's flavors. They wanted to make something with Threadgill's name on the carton in order to help introduce themselves to Texans, who already knew about us. Sandra made the motion that we invent rather than suggest, so we turned to Ben & Jerry's ice cream cookbook. We rented a five-gallon, hand-cranked ice cream freezer from Callahan's General Store. We made enough of Ben & Jerry's Sweet Cream Base for three gallons of vanilla ice cream and added ½-inch square chunks of our pecan pie to one batch and chunks of our peach cobbler to another. We made the pie and cobbler in sheet pans so they were quite a bit shallower than normal. We were aiming for big chunks but figured we had to get our mouths around the pieces.

WHAT DOWNSIZING MEANT AT THREADGILL'S

The first 10 years or so that Threadgill's was a restaurant, it was just about impossible to sell people dessert unless they intended to split it with someone. We simply served too much food. People cleaned their plates most every time anyway. They just groaned a lot and waved away most efforts to get them to try our pies and cobblers. Then we were beset with the economic bust of the mid '80s and the yuppie fitness craze, both at the same time. Plates were coming back with mashed potatoes and turnip greens left on them, and my accountant gave me an ultimatum: Either raise the prices on the menu or find a cheaper accountant. There is only one thing scarier than raising prices and that is reducing portions. Friends said that I was nuts. One even claimed he'd pay a dollar more for smaller helpings. That same night I told the story to Glenn Bob, sitting on the porch trying to muster the courage to do what had to be done, and I heard my mother's voice. From out of the past she asked in her pretty Southern drawl: "Would y'all like second helpings?" Zounds! There was the answer, clear as 99 bottles of beer on the wall. Second helpings! There was a bit of concern around the restaurant that the pressure had made me bonkers, but I insisted that everyone listen up and follow these simple instructions. First, I got the cooks smaller spoons on the serving line and smaller platters the same shape as the ones we'd always used. Without much training effort, we cut the portions of vegetables in half but the plates still looked just as crowded. Then, the wait staff was drilled over and over again to say as they put the plates down in front of their customers: "You are welcome to second helpings on any of your vegetables. (Slight pause.) But you might want to save room for dessert." Suffering succotash! It worked like magic. Hardly anyone except UT football players and a few truckers ever asked for seconds, but everybody liked the way it sounded. Nobody had been told before in a restaurant that they could get seconds, but it sounded a little bit like lots of people's moms. Tips picked up as a result and we got miles of good word of mouth from being the only such place around. Oh, yeah. Dessert sales doubled.

Pie Crust

8 tablespoons (1 stick) margarine, softened
3 ounces shortening, room temperature
1 tablespoon sugar
1 teaspoon salt
6 tablespoons ice water
10 ounces sifted flour

Blend margarine and shortening together and chill completely before using. Dissolve sugar and salt in ice water. Lightly mix flour with margarine and shortening until crumbly. Add ice water and mix lightly and slowly until dough forms a ball. Be careful not to overmix. Divide into two and chill completely before rolling out pie shells or top crust. **Makes two pie shells or 1 top and 1 bottom crust.**

Pecan Pie

1 10-inch pie shell, unbaked
1½ cups brown sugar
4 tablespoons butter, melted
2½ tablespoons flour
5 large eggs
1⅓ cups light corn syrup
¼ cup molasses
1½ teaspoons vanilla
2½ cups pecan pieces

Preheat oven to 350°. Combine sugar, butter, flour, and eggs in a bowl and whisk together. Add the syrup, molasses, and vanilla. Whisk until smooth. Arrange the pecan pieces in the unbaked pie shell and pour liquid mixture over the nuts. They will rise to the top while the pie is baking. Bake for 50 to 60 minutes at 350° or until filling is completely set in the center. Cool on a rack for about an hour before serving. **Makes 8 servings.**

☛ Pecan Pie is my favorite dessert. Every bite takes me back to another pleasant memory of Beulah and my childhood. The small pecan pieces are much preferred over the big showy halves touted by photos. They fit into a kid's mouth better, and the pie is easier to cut. And remember, if at least one person in 10 doesn't think the pie is scorched, it is not done enough to set the crispy sweetness of the pecans and brown sugar.

BANANA PUDDING

1 1/4 cups sugar
1/4 cup cornstarch
Pinch salt
5 cups whole milk
4 egg yolks, beaten
5 tablespoons butter
2 teaspoons vanilla extract
Vanilla wafers
6 bananas in thin slices

IN THE TOP of a double boiler, combine sugar, cornstarch, and salt. Add milk and whisk until smooth. Cook over medium heat until milk is hot. To temper the egg yolks, add a cup of the hot milk mixture to the egg yolks, whisking as you pour to avoid scrambling the eggs. Return the egg/milk mixture to the double boiler, whisking as you pour. Stir frequently until custard begins to thicken and will coat the back of a wooden spoon. Remove from heat and stir in butter and vanilla. Stir until butter is melted.

COVER THE BOTTOM of a deep 2-quart bowl or casserole with a thick layer of vanilla wafers. Cover the cookies with a layer of thinly sliced bananas. Pour the custard over the cookies and bananas, covering them completely. Cover the bowl with a piece of plastic wrap placed directly on the custard to avoid the formation of a "skin" on top of the custard. Chill thoroughly before serving. For individual servings, put vanilla wafers and banana slices in the bottom of each of

10 dessert bowls, cover with hot custard, and proceed as above. **Makes 10 servings.**

☛ In the restaurant we have to prepare this old favorite in little single serving bowls. It should be made in a large bowl and left in the refrigerator overnight to mysteriously disappear by morning.

SALTY CRACKER PIE

20 saltine crackers, crushed
1 pound dates, chopped
1 cup sugar
2 cups pecans, chopped
1 teaspoon baking powder
4 egg whites, room temperature
1 teaspoon vanilla
Whipped Cream (see recipe, page 164)

PREHEAT OVEN to 350°. Combine cracker crumbs, dates, sugar, pecans, and baking powder. Beat egg whites until stiff but not dry and add vanilla. Gently fold dry ingredients into egg whites and pour into a buttered 9-inch pie pan. Bake at 350° for 30 minutes. Cool and serve with Whipped Cream. **Makes 8 servings.**

☛ This is another semi-sorta secret. The name keeps it from being a mega-hit with all but the initiated. It has a candy bar texture. When I was young, almost this same recipe was on the Ritz Cracker box. Of course it used Ritz Crackers instead of saltines and it was called Pecan Delight Pie.

MISSISSIPPI MUD CAKE

CAKE:

1 cup vegetable shortening
2 cups sugar
4 large eggs
1 1/2 cups flour
1/3 cup cocoa
1/4 teaspoon salt
1 tablespoon vanilla
1 cup pecans, chopped
1 cup miniature marshmallows

FROSTING:

12 tablespoons (1 1/2 sticks) margarine
1 pound box confectioners sugar
1/3 cup cocoa
1/3 cup evaporated milk
1 teaspoon vanilla extract
1 cup pecans, chopped

PREHEAT OVEN to 350°. Cream shortening and sugar together until light and fluffy. Add eggs, one at a time, and beat well after each addition. Sift flour, cocoa, and salt together and add to creamed mixture. Fold in vanilla and chopped pecans. Pour into greased 9x13-inch pan and bake for 30 minutes. Remove cake from oven, sprinkle the marshmallows over the hot cake, and return to oven to melt them, about 10 minutes. Prepare frosting. **Makes 12 to 16 servings.**

FOR FROSTING: Melt margarine in a heavy 2-quart saucepan. Add sugar and cocoa and stir until smooth. Stir in milk, vanilla, and pecans. Pour mixture over warm cake and let stand until completely set (about 2 hours) before serving.

☛ Another old favorite in spite of the name.

PEACH COBBLER

1½ pounds (6 sticks) butter, melted
2¼ cups unbleached white flour
2¼ cups sugar
3¾ teaspoons baking powder
½ teaspoon nutmeg
2¼ cups milk
2½ pounds frozen peaches, thawed, or 4 pounds fresh peaches, peeled and sliced

PREHEAT OVEN to 350°. Pour melted butter into the bottom of a 9x13-inch baking pan. Sift dry ingredients together and then whisk in milk until there are no lumps. Pour batter over the butter but *do not stir*. Press peach slices down into the batter. Bake, uncovered, for about 30 minutes or until the top is browned. Cover with foil and continue baking for another 30 to 45 minutes or until set in the middle. Cool on a rack before serving. Serve with homemade vanilla ice cream. **Makes 12 servings.**

☛ This recipe is quicker and lighter than the traditional lattice-topped pie crust cobbler. Momma called it Mush Cobbler sometimes and Hasty Cobbler others.

APPLE PIE

STREUSEL TOPPING:

1 cup sugar
1 cup unbleached white flour
2¼ teaspoons cinnamon
12 tablespoons (1½ sticks) butter, softened

FILLING:

1 10-inch pie shell, unbaked
1½ teaspoons cinnamon
½ teaspoon allspice
8 firm, tart apples (McIntosh, Granny Smith), peeled, cored, and sliced

¼ cup sugar
¼ cup brown sugar
½ cup unbleached white flour
¾ teaspoon nutmeg
Dash salt

PREHEAT OVEN to 350° and assemble topping before peeling apples. Combine sugar, flour, and cinnamon in a small bowl. With fingers, a fork, or a pastry cutter, work softened butter into dry mixture to form coarse crumbs. Set aside. Once apples are peeled, cored, and sliced, combine dry ingredients and toss with apple slices until well coated. Fill unbaked pie shell with apples and cover completely with topping. Bake for about 1 hour, until topping is golden and filling is bubbly. Cool on a rack before slicing. Top with vanilla ice cream. **Makes 8 servings.**

☛ What can you say about a wonderful slice of apple pie, still hot enough to melt vanilla ice cream?

BUTTERMILK PIE

1 10-inch pie shell, unbaked
3 cups sugar
¼ cup flour
½ pound (2 sticks) butter, melted
6 eggs
1 cup buttermilk
2 tablespoons water
1 teaspoon lemon juice
1 teaspoon vanilla extract

PREHEAT OVEN to 350°. Whisk the sugar and flour into the melted butter and then whisk in the eggs, one at a time. Add the liquid ingredients and mix well. Pour filling into the unbaked pie shell and place on a cookie sheet in the preheated oven. Bake for 1 hour or until filling is set in the center of the pie. Cool on a rack and then refrigerate before slicing and serving. **Makes 8 servings.**

☞ There is not a smidgen of similarity between the taste of buttermilk and the taste of this pie. Calling it Buttermilk Pie helps keep it a bit of a secret. Most folks would call it a chess pie. It is very sweet but very light. I eat it when I'm too full for dessert.

DOUBLE CHOCOLATE ICE BOX PIE

1 10-inch pie shell, baked and cooled
$2\frac{1}{2}$ sticks (about $\frac{2}{3}$ pound) butter, softened to room temperature
$1\frac{3}{4}$ cups confectioners sugar, sifted
$1\frac{1}{4}$ cups cocoa powder, sifted
2 teaspoons vanilla
7 eggs, beaten
Whipped Cream (see recipe, page 164) or Chocolate Brandy Cream (see recipe, page 162)

IN THE BOWL of an electric mixer, cream together the softened butter and the confectioners sugar until smooth. On low speed, add the sifted cocoa and beat until smooth, scraping the bottom and sides of the bowl often to ensure even mixing. Blend in the vanilla and then add the eggs a few at a time, scraping down the bottom and sides of the bowl carefully after each addition. Beat until smooth. Pour pie filling into baked and cooled pie shell and chill 2 to 4 hours before serving. Top with Whipped Cream or Chocolate Brandy Cream. **Makes 8 servings.**

☞ Kinda like a chocolate concentrate, this wonder is not for sissies.

CHOCOLATE BRANDY CREAM

$1\frac{1}{2}$ tablespoons cocoa powder
1 tablespoon confectioners sugar
1 cup heavy whipping cream
1 tablespoon brandy
$1\frac{1}{2}$ teaspoons vanilla

SIFT TOGETHER the cocoa and confectioners sugar and set aside. In a chilled bowl with chilled beaters, combine all the ingredients and beat the cream until stiff peaks begin to form. With a spoon or pastry bag fitted with a star tip, use cream to garnish slices of Double Chocolate Ice Box Pie. **Makes 8 servings.**

PUMPKIN PIE

1 10-inch pie shell, unbaked
1 pound can pumpkin pie filling
2 large eggs
1 cup sugar
2 tablespoons flour, generous
2 tablespoons nonfat dry milk, scant
$\frac{1}{2}$ teaspoon salt
$\frac{1}{2}$ teaspoon cinnamon
$\frac{1}{2}$ teaspoon ginger
$\frac{1}{2}$ teaspoon nutmeg
Dash cloves
1 tablespoon dark Karo syrup
$\frac{3}{4}$ cup plus 2 tablespoons milk
Whipped Cream (see recipe, page 164)

PREHEAT OVEN to 350°. In a mixing bowl, whisk together the pumpkin and eggs. Combine the dry ingredients and add to the pumpkin mixture. Gradually whisk in the syrup and milk and beat until mixture is smooth. Pour filling into pie shell and bake for an hour or until pie is set in the center. Cool on a rack and serve with Whipped Cream. **Makes 8 servings.**

☛ If every day was really Thanksgiving, we'd sell pumpkin pie year round.

STRAWBERRY SHORTCAKE

SHORTCAKES:

3 1/3 cups Biscuit Mix (see recipe, page 76)
1/4 teaspoon nutmeg
1/2 cup sugar
8 tablespoons (1 stick) margarine, softened
1 1/3 cups whipping cream
2 tablespoons butter, melted

FILLING:

4 pints strawberries, stemmed and sliced
1/2 cup sugar
Whipped Cream (see recipe, page 164)

PREHEAT OVEN to 350°.

FOR THE SHORTCAKES: Combine the dry ingredients in a large mixing bowl. Using your hands, work the soft margarine into the flour until there are no obvious lumps. Add the cream and work it in by hand; the mixture will be very sticky. Turn the dough out onto a lightly floured surface and knead gently until the dough is not so sticky. With a lightly floured rolling pin or your hands, roll or pat the dough into a rectangle about ½-inch thick and cut with a 3-inch biscuit cutter. Gently reroll scraps to make a total of 12 shortcakes. Place shortcakes on a cookie sheet lined with parchment (baking) paper and bake at 350° for about 15 minutes or until they are lightly browned. The shortcakes will not rise very much. Remove from the oven and brush the tops with melted butter. Cool completely before filling.

FOR THE FILLING: Wash the strawberries, remove the stems, and slice. Toss with the sugar.

TO ASSEMBLE SHORTCAKES: Split the shortcakes in half, fill with a large spoonful of strawberries, and top with a large dollop of whipped cream and a few more berries. Serve immediately. **Makes 12 servings**.

☛ The strawberry capital of Texas is Poteet. It rhymes with sweet and so does this little shortcake "biscuit." It even turns frozen berries into a perfect dessert.

SWEET POTATO HONEY PIE

1 10-inch pie shell, unbaked
1 1/3 sticks (about 11 tablespoons) margarine, softened
1 1/3 cups mashed sweet potatoes
3 tablespoons flour, scant
2 large eggs plus 2 egg yolks
2/3 cup honey
1/2 cup milk
1/3 teaspoon cinnamon
1/4 teaspoon nutmeg
1/2 teaspoon vanilla
Whipped Cream (see recipe, below)

PREHEAT OVEN to 350°. Combine soft margarine, sweet potatoes and flour in a bowl and mix well. Whisk in the remaining ingredients in order listed and pour filling into the unbaked pie shell. Bake for 1 hour or until filling is set in the middle. Cool on a rack and then refrigerate. Serve with Whipped Cream. **Makes 8 servings.**

WHIPPED CREAM

2 cups very cold whipping cream
1/2 cup confectioners sugar
1 1/2 teaspoons vanilla extract

IN A CHILLED BOWL with chilled beaters, beat the whipping cream with the confectioners sugar and vanilla until soft peaks form and the cream will hold a shape. Be careful not to make butter by whipping too long! Refrigerate.

CHOCOLATE CHIP COOKIES

½ pound granulated sugar
½ pound brown sugar
⅞ teaspoon salt
1 pound (4 sticks) margarine, softened
1 large egg
1 teaspoon vanilla extract
¾ teaspoon baking soda
3 cups unbleached flour
12 ounces semisweet chocolate chips

MIX SUGARS and salt together. Cream softened margarine with sugars until smooth. Add egg and vanilla slowly to sugar mixture. Mix until blended, scraping sides of bowl once or twice. Sift soda with flour. Add to mixture. Mix only until flour is absorbed. Fold chocolate chips into dough. Do not overmix. Drop dough by generous tablespoons and bake on parchment (baking) paper in a 350° oven for about 20 to 25 minutes. **Makes about 2½ dozen cookies.**

☛ We've been making these cookies at Threadgill's for the last 10 years or so and I don't think we've sold but a few dozen. They are real good but they aren't on the menu. We keep them sorta out of the way, not exactly hidden but not front and center, either. They are for the staff to steal. It's no fair stealing them when someone's watching. You've got to at least try to be sneaky. They are also for giving away to customers who complain that they cannot eat dessert, they just don't have room for another bite. Oops, another confession: The microwave is perfectly wonderful for heating up the chocolate chips in the cookie. They also crumble up by the dozen very well for adding to a gallon of homemade vanilla ice cream.

VANILLA ICE CREAM

2 cups sugar
1 14-ounce can Eagle Brand Condensed Milk
2 tablespoons vanilla extract
Pinch salt
6 eggs, beaten
1 pint whipping cream
Milk

MIX SUGAR, condensed milk, vanilla, salt, and eggs together. Add cream and mix well. Pour into 1-gallon ice cream freezer and add enough cold milk to fill it two-thirds full. Freeze. **Makes 1 gallon ice cream.**

☛ We multiplied this recipe by three in a five-gallon ice cream freezer. When the cream began to get a little firm we added the equivalent of two pecan pies, baked in a shallow baker's pan, chilled and cut into ½-inch squares. Then we did it again, using the same procedure with our Peach Cobbler recipe. I was Ben and Sandra was Jerry. We became very popular with all our customers who taste-tested these recipes.

STRAWBERRY-RHUBARB PIE

1 recipe Pie Crust (top and bottom) (see recipe, page 155)
1 pound strawberries, cut in half
1 pound rhubarb, diced
¼ cup cornstarch
⅓ cup cold water
1¼ cups sugar
½ teaspoon salt
5 tablespoons butter, melted
1 tablespoon milk
¼ teaspoon sugar and ¼ teaspoon cinnamon, mixed

PREPARE PIE CRUST recipe and divide in half for top and bottom crusts. Blend cornstarch and cold water until very smooth and blend in sugar, 4 tablespoons melted butter, and salt. Place strawberries and rhubarb in this mixture and let stand for 15 minutes. Use half the pie dough to make bottom crust and half to make lattice-style top crust. Brush bottom crust with remaining 1 tablespoon melted butter, fill with fruit mixture, and cover with lattice. Brush top with milk and very lightly sprinkle with sugar/cinnamon mix. Bake at 350° for about 40 minutes. **Makes 1 pie.**

☛ *Austin American-Statesman*, Tuesday, March 5, 1996:

In the movie *Michael*, a romantic comedy starring John Travolta, Andie MacDowell and William Hurt that director Nora Ephron is shooting in Austin, there is a key scene in which the virtues of pie are extolled at an Iowa diner.

Which means that Travolta, MacDowell and Hurt are going to have to eat an awful lot of pie in the 12 hours it will take to film the scene.

Which means that the pie had better be really, really good.

So, in order to find the perfect not-too-sweet, not-too-tart confection, Ephron asked some local bakers to submit their wares for a tasting. In between takes at their Round Rock soundstage, the cast and crew of *Michael* sampled 30 pies from Austin pastry chefs.

"Oh, it was a thrilling day," Ephron recalled recently. "We had the Iowa favorite, of course, which is sour cream and raisin. We had apple pie and strawberry rhubarb and blueberry and coconut cream and chocolate cream. We had lemon meringue, and a black cherry pie, and peach and banana cream. It was amazing. If you laid out those pies end to end, they would fill up our entire soundstage."

After secret ballots were cast the winner was in, and it was hands-down. "There was no question that the strawberry-rhubarb pie from Threadgill's was far and away great, which was not a complete surprise to us. We all love Threadgill's," said Ephron, who next to directing such hits as *Sleepless in Seattle* is probably best known as a consummate foodie.

In 1983, she wrote the roman à clef *Heartburn*, in which she deconstructed a marriage using a gustatory template, complete with recipes. "I tried to make a strawberry-rhubarb once, and it was not my finest hour in pies," Ephron admitted. "It's not an easy pie. The thing that was amazing about Threadgill's was that it wasn't too sweet, and the tastes and fruit in it were very discreet in the most exciting way."

Threadgill's director of food services, Sam Castro, chalks up the victory to beginner's luck. "I'd never made a rhubarb pie before," he says.

Breakfast: Sausage, Grits and Gravy

Breakfast was an important meal back in Granddad's day. But breakfast had a heart attack and you can hardly recognize it anymore. When breakfast fueled a trip to the fields it was reasonable to wolf down sausage and eggs and biscuits and gravy. A commuter ride to the office, on the other hand, doesn't even burn up a jelly doughnut.

Little cups of yogurt, little cans of juice, cereal and skim milk, these are not bad products and they make it easy to kick off the day in accordance with the Food Guide Pyramid. Neatly packaged and clearly labeled, breakfasts have become the first step to food pills.

I have a happy compromise to offer: Eat fruit and cereal, maybe toast or a muffin Monday through Friday, then treat yourself to a big brunch on Saturday or Sunday.

Though Threadgill's offers a good selection of traditional Southern items on our weekend breakfast menu, we have acknowledged the glory of Tex-Mex when it comes to breakfast food. In addition to smoked bacon, pork chops, thick, juicy sausage patties, cheese grits, biscuits, gravy and potatoes, we also offer the tortilla, cheese and chili-flavored scrambled eggs known as "migas" and we make lots of refried beans. And a pitcher of Bloody Marys.

Here are a few of our recipes for a good old-fashioned breakfast. Enjoy them on the weekend, even if instead of eating like a king in order to work like a Trojan, you are only planning to eat like a hog and go take a nap. Don't forget a Bloody Mary.

THREADGILL'S BREAKFAST EXPERIENCE

I'm often asked why Threadgill's doesn't open for breakfast anymore and I try to give as many different answers as possible. "Why ruin the best meal of the day with the worst customers? The customers are grouchy. You don't make any money off the few you do get and you are assured that they will go somewhere else for lunch and supper. They don't tip and it is the hardest time of day to keep dependable help."

It is possible that my restaurant experience with breakfast at this location is jinxed because Kenneth used up all the luck during the postwar boom of the late '40s and early '50s. When the city limits moved North past the little joint, Kenneth took it as an omen that selling gas was no longer going to be profitable enough to mess with, so he shut down the pumps and tried to expand his retail by offering canned soup for 30 cents and two bottles of Texas beer for a quarter. What a deal! Painters and drywallers crowded around his lunch counter and bar and slammed down this hearty breakfast in such numbers that for several years the biggest hour of business was from 7 to 8 A.M. every weekday morning.

FIG PRESERVES

1 gallon prepared figs
1 cup baking soda
Boiling water
8 cups sugar
1 lemon

TO PREPARE FRUIT: Select perfect figs, ripe but not mushy. Leave ⅛-inch stem. Wash. To remove the fuzz, sprinkle 1 cup baking soda over 6 quarts sound figs and add 1 gallon boiling water. Let stand 5 minutes. Drain and wash thoroughly in cold water.

TO MAKE PRESERVES: Place alternate layers of sugar and figs in a 3-gallon pot. Let stand overnight. Drain off syrup and bring it to a boil. Drop in figs a few at a time. Cook until tender, transparent, and amber-colored (about 1 to 1½ hours). Add juice of lemon. Cook 10 minutes longer. Remove figs from the syrup. Fill hot, dry, sterilized jars three quarters full with preserved fruit. Cook syrup until thick. If paraffin is to be used later, add enough syrup to fill the jar to ½-inch from the top. Close and process in boiling water bath. **Makes about 6 pints.**

☛ My daddy grew a sweet tooth on cold winter mornings that was as big as a fang. After his bacon and eggs and orange juice he wanted cane syrup or warmed fig preserves on biscuits. It was a breakfast dessert.

Whenever we visited Mississippi, we would load up on half-gallon buckets of cane syrup whether we were out of our supply back in Austin or not. We never knew how long it might be before the next trip. By the time a bucket was opened it was almost always solid sugar and had to be set in a pot of boiling water until it liquefied enough to pour.

We had a big fig tree back toward the alley and every year we tried to beat the birds to the ripening figs. We only won about one year in three but it didn't take many jars of fig preserves to last a long time. We don't have much cold weather in Austin. There are not many things as simple to make and they almost fit into Mother's "free food" category.

MIGAS

8 large eggs, beaten
4 tablespoons butter
2 cups onion, diced
1 large jalapeño pepper, seeded and minced
½ clove garlic, minced (optional)
1 tomato, diced
1 ounce cheddar cheese, grated
2 ounces restaurant style tortilla chips
2 ounces Chile con Queso (see recipe, page 185)

MELT BUTTER in 12-inch non-stick skillet. Sauté onion, jalapeño, and garlic. Add tomato and toss quickly, then add eggs and continue stirring as you would scrambled eggs. When eggs are about halfway done, put in cheddar cheese, tortilla chips, and Queso sauce. Cook until eggs are done and cheese is melted, stirring constantly. Serve with refried beans, potatoes, biscuits or tortillas, bacon, sausage. **Makes 4 servings.**

☛ The possibilities for Tex-Mex breakfasts are as endless as your imagination. Set out a variety of ingredients much like you were doing a stir-fry: chopped peppers, diced tomatoes and onion, refried beans, cooked, chopped potatoes, cooked bacon strips, cooked and crumbled chorizo sausage, grated cheddar cheese. Migas are beautiful with the green and red pieces of pepper and tomato swimming in the bright yellow of the cheesy eggs with tortilla chip pieces. Yum.

BREAKFAST TACOS

☛ Refried beans and breakfast tacos...now here's a good 'un. Breakfast tacos constitute an industry by themselves in this part of the country. Heat a flour tortilla in a skillet (or on an open flame, or in a microwave or in the oven) and roll anything good for breakfast up in it. Wrap it in foil and put in an ice chest with a hundred others, all piping hot. Pull up to a big crew of hard-working people who didn't get enough breakfast. Whammo! You're in business.

Mock Hash Brown Potatoes

2 pounds Idaho potatoes
3 ounces oil or 6 tablespoons melted butter
2 teaspoons paprika
Salt and pepper

Boil potatoes and chill. Peel and dice into ¼-inch pieces. Cover bottom of skillet with small amount of oil or butter. Arrange a single layer of diced potatoes on the bottom of the skillet. Drizzle with a small amount of oil or butter, then sprinkle with paprika and cook till almost crisp. Flip with spatula. Dust lightly again with paprika. Remove when crisp. Season with salt and pepper.

Note: For use in breakfast tacos, just warm up the potatoes in a skillet or on a griddle after breaking up.

Spinach Omelets

12 eggs
4 tablespoons butter
2 cups Spinach Casserole (see recipe, page 110)
1 cup Gruyère cheese, grated

Heat 1 tablespoon of butter in omelet pan. Beat 3 eggs well and pour into hot butter. Cook until set. Add ¼ of Spinach Casserole and ¼ cup cheese. Fold omelet and cook until done to desired firmness. Repeat for 4 individual omelets. Serve with toast and tomatoes.

EGGS FLORENTINE

12 eggs
2 tablespoons Pernod (optional)
2 cups Spinach Casserole (see recipe, page 110)

POACH THE EGGS. Divide the spinach evenly among 6 plates. Make a depression in the top of the spinach with the back of a large spoon. Place 2 poached eggs in each portion of the spinach. Drizzle Pernod over all. Serve for brunch over toast. **Makes 6 servings**.

☛ These are two of many ways to use the Spinach Casserole recipe but the only ones I use in the morning.

Song to Bacon

by Roy Blount, Jr.

Consumer groups have gone and taken
Some of the savor out of bacon.
Protein-per-penny in bacon, they say,
Equals needles-per-square-inch of hay.
Well, I know, after cooking all
That's left to eat is mighty small
(You also get a lot of lossage
In life, romance and country sausage),
And I will vote for making it cheaper,
Wider, longer, leaner, deeper,
But let's not throw the baby, please.
Out with the (visual rhyme here) grease.
There's nothing crumbles like bacon still,
And I don't think there ever will
Be anything, whate'er you use
For meat, that chews like bacon chews.
Also, I'd like these groups to tell
Me whether they factored in the smell.
The smell of it cooking's worth $2.10 a pound.
And how 'bout the sound*?*

HOLD'JA OVERS AND SPIRITUALS

For years I made flip remarks to customers that if they wanted appetizers they were in the wrong place. If you aren't hungry, why in the world would you be at Threadgill's? Or maybe, "It will be about 20 minutes for a table. Our version of an appetizer." Yuk, yuk. Threadgill's is a place to bring an enormous appetite. Even if you are on a serious diet and are planning to eat nothing but vegetables, it only makes sense to eat as many as you can when you have the rare opportunity to choose from so very large a selection.

But times change. We cut the vegetable portions in half and began to offer second helpings. That caused the explosion in the demand for desserts. Next, our friends in Lubbock at Dynamic Foods learned how to mass-produce breaded green tomato slices and dill pickle spears so that the batter stays on in the deep fryer. Then I sponsored the Armadillo World Headquarters reunion and the famous nachos had to be revived, never to die again.

Then the obvious happened when we began trying to get customers to frequent the joint on the way home for "Howdy Hour." (It had long been a Texas tradition, learned in Southern Louisiana most likely, to give folks several inexpensive drinks before they drive home after work. All over the

FRIED
UNGENTLEMANLY OR UNLADYLIKE CONDUCT WILL NOT BE TOLERATED IN THIS ESTABLISHMENT
We will not serve minors nor permit them to consume any Alcoholic Beverage on the premises
We observe legal opening and closing hours
We reserve the right to refuse service to anyone
We will not permit vulgarity, profanity, excessive noise or other evidence of misbehavior
We intend to protect our license and your privilege to enjoy your beer by insisting that the laws and regulations be observed
CO-OPERATION WILL BE APPRECIATED
The Proprietor
Shiner

state, gasoline and beer are sold in great volume at the same stores. Some even carry ammo.) Already on our menu were fried chicken livers and fried oysters. They're both hard to beat with a cold pitcher of beer. It was easy to cut our cutlets and our chicken breast into strips and fry them up on a platter with a bowl of cream gravy on the side. Even so, we still seem to have a different purpose than most restaurants when it comes to appetizers. Rather than to tantalize the appetite, we serve them as small meals that help postpone a larger meal. They are more like large snacks. We serve them to "hold'ja over" till you get home for supper.

In the Museum there is a collection of the few items that Kenneth used to provide "hold'ja over" nourishment to his beer-drinking patrons. Snacks would be a kind description. (Imagine Bessie Smith on the jukebox wailing, "Gimme a pig's foot and a bottle of beer." Lena Horne and LaVerne Baker recorded it too. That song must have sold a million pigs' feet. I'll bet it made an impression on Janis.) He made a terribly hot mustard, and he kept it in a butcher case with a big block of cheddar cheese. On a big lazy Susan in the center of the bar were a collection of gallon jars that held pigs' feet, pickled eggs, beer sausage and jerky, peanuts and saltines. Hanging in easy reach above these jars was a Frito rack with various kinds of chips. He claimed that Frito Corn Chips was the first popular Tex-Mex food 'cause the recipe had been purchased from a Mexican lady in San Antonio. Many years later I realized that his saltines, cheese and mustard, when combined, made a honky nacho. Anything that was spicy hot, fried, salty, and cheesy certainly went well with a cold beer. Hors d'oeuvres have gotten a lot more sophisticated, but the key elements are still the same and most of them sit right up at the tip top of the Food Guide Pyramid.

This is the most appropriate place to make a few Spiritual notes. The subject of alcoholic beverages is a bit touchy in a book dedicated to the memory of Beulah. Mother never had the first sip of such. She never even developed a taste for coffee. Her worst nightmare was that I'd end up hanging out in beer joints and wind up a bum. Sure enough, the first thing I did after getting fired from my schoolteaching job was get a job as a P.R. lobbyist for the United States Brewer's Association. At least it paid better than teaching and I wore a suit. It was as a lobbyist that I learned to recite that beer is "the beverage of moderation" and a whole spiel about the fact that mankind has been creating ways to get crocked since about the same time as we began experimenting with fire.

From the Brewer's Association I went straight into promoting musical events performed and attended by folks with long hair who, it was rumored, tended to do worse than drink beer. Even so, the place where these events occurred, Armadillo World Headquarters, became known for a while as the biggest "full service honky-tonk and beer joint in all of Texas." In spite of her fears, Mother was ferociously proud of how we hippies struggled against the odds, worked hard to produce good shows and seemingly held our beer at least as well as young German philosophy scholars.

Lo and behold, I went from the biggest beer joint in Texas to the oldest beer joint in Austin, in just one fell swoop. Kenneth Threadgill stood in line all night to get the first beer license issued in Travis County upon the repeal of "the noble experiment." He ran his little place as a family business for 40 years, through 1974. By 1979, when I set about turning Threadgill's old, dilapidated and deserted building into a family restaurant, Mother could laugh at my inclination to end up in a roomful of happy folks, toasting the journey instead of the destination.

By most accounts the behavior of our pioneer cowboys and mercenaries gave plenty of justification to the ideals of the temperance movement. In her fine book, *Notes on the Republic*, Ellen Murry quotes a British traveler, Francis Sheridan, who remarked on the Texans' favorite avocation in 1840: "The passion for erecting grog shops supersedes the thirst of religious worship and Temples wherein to exercise it, for though we find every town plentifully supplied with Pot-Houses (taverns or grog shops), we see neither a church or signs of building one." Everything in their rigorous life encouraged drinking, from their fear of water to their diet of meats preserved by heavy salting. There were too few women available to expect much in the way of a domestic society. The scant available womenfolk certainly saw enough alcohol-fueled violence to make them easy recruits for Carrie Nations.

John Herndon, who visited Texas in 1837, admitted that "there is something relaxing in the climate that makes it necessary for all to indulge in the use of some kind of stimulus to some extent to keep up the spirits." He observed: "...a large majority knew no restraint to their appetites. The extent to which this vice was carried exceeded all belief. It appeared to be the business of the great mass of the people to collect around these centers of vice and hold their drunken orgies, without seeming to know that the Sabbath was made for more serious purposes and the night for rest." At this time Houston had 47 establishments for selling intoxicating drinks. The records at the clerk's office for Fort Bend County indicate that between 1838 and 1846, more licenses were issued for the retail sale of wines and spiritous liquors than for all other businesses combined.

The effect of corn, the principal ingredient in whiskey (often called the American wine), on temperance was strong. By the time German immigrants had established their first lager breweries, mostly in San Antonio, the temperance movement was gaining momentum. It took a hundred years to win their war but already by the time of the Republic its members were pushing for total abstinence, including beer and wine, which had been previously excluded. When a recruit agreed to abstain from all alcohol, a "T" was placed against his name for "total." Even Sam Houston reportedly signed a pledge to become a "teetotaler" at a meeting of the Temperance Society in 1839, which was attended by 89 *drunkards*. Some say he would never have done so had he not been drunk. And needless to say, the pledge didn't take.

Texas breweries lost their charters to brew a couple of years before Prohibition felled the national brands. The Texas Attorney General brought a successful suit against all of them except the little Spoetzel Brewery in Shiner in 1916 for restraint-of-trade and poll-tax violations. The suit alleged that price fixing and de facto ownership of the majority of the Texas breweries by the big Yankee Pabst and German Busch brewing families constituted a very un-American atmosphere. Cosmo Spoetzel continued brewing beer in Shiner until he got busted with a big load in Galveston and spent a year in prison. The Pearl Brewery in San Antonio switched to the making of near beer and soda water, as did Anheuser-Busch in Milwaukee. Sabinas Brewing moved across the border into Matamoros, Mexico, and continued brewing for the express purpose of smuggling its products back into the U.S.

By the end of Prohibition, some of those who had the strongest motivation to continue it were bootleggers. East Texas was full of moonshiners who helped "dry" forces win local option elections in order to protect their proprietary grip on the sale of spirits.

Kenneth Threadgill was a facilitator for those who would not be denied their grog ration. Some folks said bootlegger was a more appropriate title. As a spirited young wag graduating from Austin High School in 1928, his motto, stated in the yearbook, was, "It is not so important to get to do what you want to do as it is to enjoy doing what you have to do." It seemed that Kenneth was assigned by nature the tasks of telling stories, singing songs, and, in order to begin the job of raising a family, selling a bit of bootleg whiskey.

When Kenneth began selling legal beer in 1933 there was a lot of pride around here in selling Texas products. Pearl and Lone Star, Grand Prize, Southern Select and Shiner all put up a good struggle against the national brands into the '60s. Gradually, though, they began to feel the economic pinch of competition with the Goliaths. Falstaff and Schlitz and Carling and other national powers gradually succumbed to the advertising might of Anheuser-Busch, Miller and Coors. One of the few good outcomes of the yuppification of the baby boomers is the explosion of imported beer of quality into the U.S. It has been caused, in part, by the realization that three good-tasting beers cause a better buzz than a dozen "lite" tasting beers and the end result is less alcohol. (A similar pattern is emerging in the return of glass-bottled milk. As more people realize they should drink less milk because of its fat and cholesterol content, they are determined to drink better milk.) In a perfect world, all beer would be draught, drunk from clean glasses or mugs stored at the same temperature as the beer. Frost causes a watering down of the beer. The popularity of frosted mugs arose from campuses. Youngsters wanted to get high on beer even though they didn't like the taste. Ice cold beer in frosted mugs helped achieve their buzz without the hearty taste to slow them down.

Canned beer ranks right down below canned spinach for yucky, especially if the beer is consumed straight from the can. The early cans might have tasted even worse from the taste of metal, but at least they had a cone top and were sealed with a beer bottle cap. Its removal allowed a clean surface to touch the lips. The flat-top cans of today have a rim around the edge that couldn't have been better designed to catch dust and any other form of filth that has a chance to settle on the surface. It is next to impossible to pour beer from a can and not wash some trash off with the beer. When any beer is packaged into cans or bottles, carbon dioxide is forced into the container as well. When you pour the brew into a glass, the foamy head that forms on top is, in part, the release of that carbon dioxide. When you pour beer straight from a can into your mouth, that carbon dioxide has no place to go but into you. Therefore, the bloated feeling that sometimes accompanies the consumption of a couple of beers is more likely to occur if the beer is drunk straight from a can.

The longneck bottle was an ingenious invention. Its neck is a compartment full of air that serves as a removal system for that gas-filled foam. Open a longneck and take a sip. Go ahead, tilt its bottom all the way up, take a little sip, then set it down on the bar. Look at the head form in the neck. The air traveled to the bottom of the bottle when it was raised and back to the neck when it was lowered. That caused the beer to give up a large portion of the carbon dioxide into a frothy head that now bubbles up into the neck. It's been released into the bottle instead of into you. Of course, if you are not in a seedy little bar with no dishwasher or standing about the chili pot in the great outdoors, the thing to strive for is a clean beer glass. Pour up your brew and let it sit a moment or two while a million bubbles burst. Put a quarter in the jukebox and sit a spell.

Speaking of little glasses... there is a piece of bygone icehouse beer drinking format that I miss from time to time. In the Museum at Threadgill's there is a collection of little glasses with printed beer brand logos. Some of them are multicolored, some even have gold rims. They are quite fancy by today's standards, and they have become extinct in the last couple of decades. I call them barrel glasses because of their shape. They used to provide a nice audio diversion in a roadhouse when a waitress carried a tray of longnecks across the room with the clean little glasses turned upside down over the freshly opened bottles. The resulting tinkle, tinkle, tinkle was a beer joint's sleigh bell. There's no telling how many extra bottles of beer were drunk because of the little glasses. You see, they held 5½ ounces of beer. Actually, because of the foam on the first one poured, it held less than that. Now a bottle of beer in Texas, back in those days, by law was always 12 ounces. You figure. The last pour that emptied the bottle into the glass was always just a tiny bit, usually less than half a glass, a very little sip. No matter how many bottles had already been emptied, that last tiny sip was somehow just not quite enough. Sure, go ahead. Bring me one more. (I'll bet it was just this kind of insidious scheming that Momma was concerned about getting me hooked. And you know, she was almost right.)

BLOODY MARY

1½ shots favorite vodka per drink
1 46-ounce can tomato juice
½ bottle (5 fluid ounces) Worcestershire sauce
½ tablespoon celery salt
1 tablespoon pepper
4 dashes Tabasco Sauce

GARNISH with lemon and lime. **Makes 10 5-ounce drinks.**

☛ Some mornings, especially Sunday mornings, it used to be hard to get up without deciding first on whether to sing a Kris Kristofferson tune or a Willie Nelson tune in the shower.

THREADGILL'S MARGARITA

1½ ounces tequila
¾ ounce triple sec
3 ounces sweet and sour mix (Good Spirits Lemon)
1 ounce freshly squeezed lime juice
Splash orange juice
1 lime wedge
Coarse-ground salt

POUR MARGARITA SALT or other coarse-ground salt on small plate. Rub the rim of a cocktail glass with a lime wedge and dip the rim of the glass until it is coated with salt. Fill the cocktail glass with ice cubes. Fill a mixing glass with cracked ice. Add the tequila, triple sec, lime juice, sweet and sour, and orange juice. Shake and strain into the cocktail glass. Garnish with the lime wedge. **Makes 1 drink.**

☛ Jimmy Buffet is about as nice a guy as ever played the Armadillo and I never drink a margarita without toasting him the best of health.

PITCHER OF THREADGILL'S MARGARITAS

1 1/3 cups tequila
1/2 cup triple sec
2 1/2 cups sweet and sour mix (Good Spirits Lemon)
3/4 cup freshly squeezed lime juice
3 ounces orange juice
7 lime wedges
Coarse-ground salt

POUR ALL INGREDIENTS except lime wedges into a 48-ounce pitcher. Stir well. Salt rims of glasses and fill with ice. Pour mixture over ice. Garnish with lime wedges. **Makes about 7 Margaritas.**

☞ When a good cause uses the Upstairs Store to raise money I try to help by mixing our margaritas in pitchers. We call these Fun Raisers.

ARMADILLO WORLD HEADQUARTERS NACHOS

12 6-inch fried corn tortillas (tostadas)
3 cups Refried Beans (see recipe, page 97)
12 ounces cheddar cheese, grated
6 ounces pickled jalapeño peppers, sliced

SPREAD each tortilla with 2 tablespoons hot refried beans (similar to peanut butter) and sprinkle on 1 ounce cheese. Top with pepper slices. Bake in 350° oven about 3 minutes. **Makes 12 nachos (4 to 6 servings).**

☞ During my early youth I lived on a wonderful combination of fuels provided by peanut butter sandwiches and large glasses of milk.

During my middle youth in the '70s I switched fuels. An Aus-Tex version of the Tex-Mex nacho was developed at the Armadillo World Headquarters. It enabled us to provide a hearty dose of nutrients (corn tortilla and pinto beans combined to form a whole protein) at a good value (we undercharged for everything and yet, like all good hippies, we worried constantly that we charged too much). The jalapeño slices that topped the nacho certainly helped decide the lubricant of choice: cold beer and lots of it. Milk became a beverage of the morning. Frisbee food, our nachos were sometimes called. Not only because of their large size and round shape but because they were so tempting to sail across the beer garden when hunger had been satisfied and too much had been drunk.

We used to put the round slices of jalapeño on top of the cheese; that made it easy for the weenies to pick them off. My cooks place them on top of the beans and under the cheese. They have no intention of removing the peppers and it better spreads the flavor.

Conventional nachos are smaller, the size of dipping chips. To be made properly they require a lot of time and attention, each one needing separate assembly. They can be much faster to eat than to make and I've seen assembly line efforts take on the drudgery of a computer chip factory. As an arena snack food, nachos have been disgraced beyond recognition. Melted Cheese Whiz poured willy-nilly over a paper boat full of chips is the common treatment nowadays. Shame. That's why we took the chip out of nacho. The way we would slap the big 'uns together was more like making open-faced peanut butter sandwiches. It was an assembly line, for sure. But we were creating real food in large-sized handfuls. Sophistication shrinks before the appetites of the masses. No teensy weensy, no curled-up pinkie. Bites as big as you wanted to try: corn, beans, cheese and peppers. Yum.

FRIED GREEN TOMATOES

Green tomatoes
Bread crumbs
***Frying* oil**
Buttermilk dressing
Dry ice (optional)

SLICE FIRM green tomatoes just over ¼-inch thick. Coat with bread crumbs. Cover baking pan with breaded slices. Top with another pan turned upside down. Place a block of dry ice on top for a minute. Move to another location for another minute. Repeat until the breaded slices are frozen solid. Fry until done. Store them in your freezer and repeat until you have at least 4 or 5 slices for each person you expect to serve. Serve with buttermilk dressing. **Makes, uh, how many tomatoes you got?**

☛ To fry food in your home kitchen you either have to love fried foods or some person who does, completely out of proportion to logic and good health. It has been said that you show love by the size of mess you are willing to make and then clean. Frying foods is a test of the mess you are willing to make. I will try to give a few tips to help with your mess control. Like juggling and jumping rope, you can do it often enough to become good and efficient. In the process, however, you will drop lots of stuff that'll need picking up and you will get very tired of doing it before you get very good. The little fellows just fall apart in the oil.

The breading falls off and leaves you feeling clumsy, like you've got little doorknobs on the ends of your fingers. You're standing over the heat of a blacksmith's forge and you need the tweezers of a seamstress. But there is a secret if you are willing to go to the trouble. Freeze the slices of breaded green tomatoes. Then you can treat 'em like hockey pucks and they'll stay together just fine. I even invented a dry ice method of freezing enough for a church supper or a big fish-fry. Dry ice is not as dangerous as hot grease but it can get you if you don't watch out. Ideally, these would be served as a vegetable, but they are so much trouble to prepare that I encourage people to use them as appetizers so I can charge more.

CHILE CON QUESO

1½ pounds Velveeta, cubed
1 10-ounce can cream of celery soup
4 ounces green chilies, diced
1 tomato, diced
½ cup yellow onion, diced
2 tablespoons jalapeño peppers, seeded and minced
½ cup picante sauce, medium hot

PLACE WATER in bottom of 2-quart double boiler and preheat. Combine all ingredients in top of boiler and cook over medium heat, stirring as needed. It will take about 40 minutes to get to serving temperature. Serve hot with fresh tortilla chips. **Makes 1½ quarts.**

☛ Try a bit of Chile con Queso on anything short of dessert.

CHICKEN-FRIED STRIPS (CHICKEN OR BEEF)

2 pounds boneless, skinless chicken breasts
***Frying* oil**
1 egg, beaten
1 cup milk
1 tablespoon Poultry Seasoning (see recipe, page 38)
1½ cups flour

HEAT 2 INCHES of oil in a skillet to 325°. Mix egg and milk. Cut chicken into strips ½-inch wide and sprinkle seasoning on top. Bread strips, dipping them in flour, then egg mix, and back into the flour. Carefully place half of the strips into hot oil and cook about 3 minutes. Turn over and cook for one minute more. Keep warm and cook rest of chicken or beef strips. Drain on a platter lined with paper towels and serve with Cream Gravy or Jalapeño Honey Mustard or ranch dressing as dip.

☛ Use either boneless, skinless chicken breasts or beef cutlets.

FRIED CHICKEN LIVERS

1 pound chicken livers
***Frying* oil**
1 egg, beaten
½ cup milk
1 cup flour
1 teaspoon salt
1 teaspoon black pepper

HEAT 2 INCHES of oil in a skillet to 325°. Mix egg and milk. Mix flour, salt, and pepper. Dip chicken livers into egg mixture and then into flour. Place chicken livers into hot oil extremely slowly and carefully. Be very careful when you cook these delights because they will pop very hot oil out of the pan very quickly and a very long distance. Cover the skillet with a lid, and after 4 or 5 minutes use 12-inch tongs to turn the livers over. Cover again and cook for 4 more minutes. Remove livers to a platter lined with paper towels to drain. Serve with Cream Gravy.

☛ This is one of our most popular entrées. The cooks hate them because they splatter and pop unreasonably, so they fight back by serving more chicken livers in a bigger pile than you've ever seen or even heard about. It seems kinda like they think they are going to make everyone regret ordering them. On the other hand, they only cost us about 65 cents a pound, and we are very proud of giving customers exceptional value.

STUFFED MUSHROOM CAPS

☛ Our wonderful Bill Arnold recipe for Spinach Casserole again (see recipe, page110). Stuffed into large mushroom caps, it has been passed off as pretty fancy fare in some mighty fine Dallas mansions. There's nothing to it once you've concocted a batch of the casserole. Heat the casserole first or not, it's not important. Scoop a reasonable amount into large caps placed on a baking tray and place in a 350° oven for about 5 minutes. They can be done in a microwave or even under a broiler if you are careful and watch closely. They don't take long, and they can be prepared in massive quantities ahead of large gatherings and held in the refrigerator until ready to heat up.

STUFFED JALAPEÑOS

24 pickled jalapeño peppers, slit and deseeded
2 cups cheddar cheese, grated
2 cups Monterey Jack cheese, grated
1 egg
2 cups whole milk
1 cup masa harina (specialty cornmeal)
2 cups flour
***Frying* oil**

BLEND grated cheeses together. Stuff each jalapeño with cheese mixture. Beat egg and mix with milk for egg wash. Combine crumbs and masa harina. Roll stuffed peppers in flour, dip into egg wash, and roll in crumb mixture. Freeze peppers until needed. Heat frying oil to 325° and fry peppers for about 2 minutes until golden brown and cheese is melted. Drain on a platter lined with paper towels. Serve with ranch dressing or Jalapeño Honey Mustard.

☛ This whole category of the cookbook is usually known as snack food and it is a huge national market in the billions of dollars. There is nothing wrong with a little Hold'ja Over. It is just a shame when folks get hooked on anything to the exclusion of the good things they really need.

The worst of the low-fat-shuckster jive is taking place in this category and the breakthroughs are important. Oh Lord, save us from olestra! Fried chips dipped into fatty dips are now having to compete with baked chips dipped into no-fat dips. And the country gets fatter. Lite, Dry, Ice beer and no-fat snacks, and the country gets fatter.

Song to Eggs

by Roy Blount, Jr.

Our best-laid plans will yield to fate.
And we will say, "We lived. We ate."

THREADGILL'S

COMIC BOOK

Being a Short History of Kenneth Threadgill, His Beer Joint, and the Live Music Capital of the World, Austin, Texas.

WRITTEN and ILLUSTRATED BY

JACK JACKSON

LETTERED BY PATRICK OWSLEY

PRODUCED BY EDDIE WILSON

HIS AUSTIN HIGH SCHOOL SENIOR YEARBOOK (1928) PROCLAIMED KENNETH'S MOTTO: "THE SECRET OF HAPPINESS IS NOT IN DOING WHAT ONE LIKES, BUT IN LIKING WHAT ONE HAS TO DO."

THE ENCOUNTER CHANGED KENNETH THREADGILL'S LIFE.

IN 1929, KENNETH MARRIED MILDRED GREER.

FROM THEIR FILLING STATION AT 6416 NORTH LAMAR (KNOWN THEN AS THE DALLAS HIGHWAY) THEY SOLD GAS OUT THE FRONT DOOR, BOOZE OUT THE BACK DOOR, DURING THE PROHIBITION YEARS.

THE BEER JOINT ATTRACTED PICKERS AND SINGERS FOR LATE NIGHT GAMBLING AND JAMMING AFTER THEIR REGULAR DANCE HALL GIGS WERE OVER.

I'M WAITING FOR SHIPS THAT NEVER COME IN...

THE OUTBREAK OF WORLD WAR II PUT A DAMPER ON THE MUSIC SCENE AT THREADGILL'S.
DEAD AROUND HERE TONIGHT... MIGHT AS WELL CLOSE.
GULF

KENNETH WORKED FOR THE CORPS OF ENGINEERS ON JOBS IMPORTANT ENOUGH TO DEFER HIS I-A DRAFT STATUS AND KEEP HIM OUT OF THE ARMY.

BUSINESS PICKED UP AFTER THE WAR AND AUSTIN BEGAN TO GROW; SO DID KENNETH'S FAMILY.
TRAFFIC ON THIS HIGHWAY SHORE IS GETTIN' WORSE.
YES, IT SURE IS...

BY THE TIME THE CITY OF AUSTIN ANNEXED HIS PLACE IN 1948, KENNETH HAD DECIDED TO QUIT PUMPING GAS AND JUST SELL BEER.
WANT SOME RAT CHEESE AND CRACKERS TO GO WITH IT?
YEAH, AND ONE OF THEM PICKLED PIG'S FEET.
FALSTAFF
JAX BEER
10 JUNE
CIGARS

HE AND MILDRED WORKED IN SHIFTS. HE OPENED AROUND 6:30 A.M. AND WENT TILL NOON. THEN MILDRED TOOK OVER WHILE HE NAPPED.
YOU'RE STARTING EARLY TODAY, SLIM...
KEEPS ME YOUNG AND FRISKY.
KEN, I'M ABOUT CLEANED UP HERE.
BE OUT DRECKLY...
IN THE LATE AFTERNOONS AND EVENINGS, KENNETH WOULD PLAY HIS STACK OF 78s AND SWAP STORIES ABOUT THE BLUE YODELER, JIMMIE RODGERS.
NOW, BACK IN '28 WHEN I WUZ TAKING TICKETS AT LOEW'S...
SOME SAY THAT'S WHEN THE WEDNESDAY NIGHT TRADITION BEGAN.
ALL AROUND TH' WATER TANK, WAITING FOR A TRAIN...

MEANWHILE, OVER IN THE HYDE PARK NEIGHBORHOOD, BEULAH WILSON WAS STARTING A DAY NURSERY.

EDDIE WILSON AND HIS MOM HAPPENED TO BE DOWNTOWN AT SEARS ONE DAY WHEN A SALES-MAN WAS DEMONSTRATING A NEW GADGET.

UNBEKNOWNST TO YOUNG EDDIE, HIS FUTURE WAS ABOUT TO BE PREORDAINED.

EDDIE WILSON LOVED HIS VEGGIES AFTER DRAWING -- YOU GUESSED IT! -- HIS MOTHER'S TICKET FROM THE JAR.

IN LATER YEARS AT McCALLUM HIGH, EDDIE MET KENNETH THREADGILL'S DAUGHTER DOTTIE.

THUS DID A TEEN-AGED EDDIE WILSON DISCOVER THREADGILL'S BEER JOINT, HANGING AROUND IN HOPES OF SPARKIN' DOTTIE.

AT THE UNIVERSITY OF TEXAS EDDIE MET STAN ALEXANDER, HIS FRESHMAN ENGLISH TEACHER WHO WENT TO THREADGILL'S FOR ANOTHER REASON.

THE HILLBILLY MUSIC PLAYED BY THE LOCALS AT THREADGILL'S SHARED THE "STAGE" WITH THE UT STUDENTS ATTEMPTS AT AN AUTHENTIC EARLY BLUEGRASS SOUND.

BUT THERE WERE OTHER "FOLKIES" AT UT NOT AS CLEAN-CUT AS STAN ALEXANDER'S GROUP.

THEY WERE KNOWN AS THE GHETTO CROWD, AFTER A RUN-DOWN APARTMENT COMPLEX AT 2812½ NUECES STREET.

...AND THEN DRIFT OVER TO THE GHETTO OR SOME OTHER PAD AND CAROUSE TILL THE WEE HOURS.

IN 1963, TO GET RID OF THIS MOTLEY CREW, UT MADE BEER DRINKING IN THE UNION ILLEGAL.

SO THE FREAKS DECIDED TO TRANSFER THEIR FOLK SINGS TO THREADGILL'S BEER JOINT.

NOBODY WAS SURE IF THE "REDNECKS" WOULD SUFFER LONGHAIRS IN THEIR MIDST. MOST OTHER PLACES IN AUSTIN WOULDN'T--

KENNETH RECOGNIZED HER TALENT AND ENCOURAGED HER TO DEVELOP IT, BECOMING ALMOST A FATHER FIGURE TO HER.

MILDRED ALSO TOOK JANIS UNDER HER WING.

A LONGHAIRED POET NAMED CHET HELMS GOT TURNED ON TO JANIS' SINGING AT ONE OF THE THREADGILL'S SESSIONS.

EDDIE WILSON WAS ANOTHER REGULAR AT THE BEER JOINT, BECAUSE OF ITS ICE COLD BEER AND FOOT-STOMPIN' MUSIC.

IN THE MID-60s, THE FOLK CROWD GRADUALLY DRIFTED AWAY FROM THREADGILL'S. GREATER EVENTS BECKONED ON THE WEST COAST.

CHET REMEMBERED JANIS (WHO HAD ALREADY MADE THE LOCAL COFFEE HOUSE SCENE) AND LURED HER OUT TO THE COAST AGAIN.

HER APPEARANCE WITH BIG BROTHER AT THE MONTERREY POP FESTIVAL IN JUNE 1967 LAUNCHED JANIS ON THE ROAD TO FAME AND FORTUNE.

BACK IN AUSTIN, KENNETH THREADGILL WAS TAKING HIS SINGING SERIOUSLY. HE FORMED A BAND, THE HOOTENANNY HOOTS, AND BEGAN TO YODEL AT CLUBS LIKE THE SPLIT RAIL.

DURING THE LATE '60s, KENNETH PLAYED THE NEWPORT FOLK FESTIVAL, BUMPING INTO AN "OLD" FRIEND.

JANIS NEVER FORGOT KENNETH, NOR DID HE FORGET HER. WHEN JULY 10, 1970, WAS PROCLAIMED KENNETH THREADGILL DAY, JANIS CANCELLED A CONCERT IN HAWAII TO SHOW UP AT HIS "JUBILEE" IN OAK HILL.

ABOUT THAT TIME, EDDIE WILSON, THE FLEDGLING MANAGER OF A ROCK GROUP NAMED SHIVA'S HEADBAND, DECIDED TO OPEN A MUSIC HALL IN WHAT HAD FORMERLY BEEN A NATIONAL GUARD ARMORY, LOCATED BEHIND A SKATING RINK.
I DON'T THINK ANYBODY WILL BE ABLE TO FIND THIS PLACE.
I'D RATHER IT BE HIDDEN OVER HERE THAN IN THE MIDDLE OF CONGRESS AVENUE.
SKATING PA
THE VULCAN GAS COMPANY HAD CLOSED ON CONGRESS AVENUE A FEW MONTHS EARLIER, AND AUSTIN'S LUNATIC FRINGE WAS WITHOUT A SPACIOUS PLACE TO BOOGIE.
VULCAN GAS COMPANY
ROCK
DANCES
LIGHTSHOWS
FOR LEASE
STOKES REALTY
458-9173
THUS WAS BORN THE ARMADILLO WORLD HEADQUARTERS, ONE OF THE MOST MIND-BOGGLING CREATIVE OPERATIONS TEXAS HAS EVER SEEN.
SHIVA'S HEADBAND
ARMADILLO
HUB CITY MOVERS
WHISTLER
AUG 7-8
FRIDAY SAT
DANCE CONCERT
WORLD HEADQUARTERS
525½ BARTON SPRINGS ROAD (REAR.)
BEHIND THE SKATING PALACE

PLUS, THE AWHQ EVENTUALLY OBTAINED SOMETHING THE VULCAN NEVER HAD.

THE MURALS AND POSTERS BY JIM FRANKLIN -- A HOLDOVER FROM VULCAN DAYS -- AND OTHER TALENTED ARTISTS GAVE THE 'DILLO A UNIQUE TEXAS FLAVOR.

OVER THE YEARS, A KITCHEN AND BEER GARDEN WERE ADDED.

IT GOT A REPUTATION AS NOT ONLY A GOOD PLACE TO HEAR MUSIC BUT A MELLOW PLACE TO HANG OUT.
SURE BEATS L.A., DON'T IT?
SURE DOES!

THE AWHQ BOOKED ALL KINDS OF ACTS, FROM BETTE MIDLER, BRUCE SPRINGSTEEN, JIMMY CLIFF, FRANK ZAPPA, COMMANDER CODY, FREDDIE KING, VAN MORRISON, TAJ MAHAL, MOSE ALLISON, MANCE LIPSCOMB, THE POINTER SISTERS...
TO PONTIFICATE NO LONGER AND TO CEASE ANY FURTHER ADO, TO MAKE YOU WISER AND HIPPER, THE AWHQ PRESENTS TO YOU--DR. JOHN THE NITE TRIPPER!

OF COURSE, KENNETH PLAYED THE AWHQ TOO--SOUNDING BETTER THAN EVER AND ATTRACTING A NEW CROP OF FANS. LIKE THEM, HE LET HIS HAIR GROW LONGER.

IN 1972, WITH THE HELP OF KRIS KRISTOFFERSON, KENNETH CUT AN ALBUM IN NASHVILLE. IT FELL INTO ONE OF THOSE BLACK HOLES.

EDDIE AND THE 'DILLO CREW LATER HELPED ORGANIZE WILLIE'S FIRST 4th OF JULY PICNIC AT DRIPPING SPRINGS.
WILL THE CIRCLE BE UNBROKEN...
CAN YOU BELIEVE THIS IS HAPPENING?
NOPE-- NEVER THOUGHT I'D SEE TH' DAY.

WILLIE LIKED THE LAID-BACK SCENE. WHEN HE SPREAD THE WORD, MANY OF HIS NASHVILLE FRIENDS FLOCKED TO AUSTIN TO PLAY AND HANG OUT. OTHERS FOLLOWED THE MIGRATION.
BOYS, THEY KEEP TELLING ME THAT THIS IS TEXAS, BUT I THINK WE MUST HAVE DIED AND GONE TO HEAVEN.
SOAP CREEK SALOON

FROM THIS UNLIKELY FUSION OF REBEL COUNTRY-AND-WESTERN WITH THE ARMADILLO'S HIPPIE MENTALITY CAME THE "COSMIC COWBOY" PHENOMENON. AUSTIN SHOT TO THE FOREFRONT AS THE LIVE MUSIC CAPITAL OF AMERICA.
I JUST WANNA BE A COSMIC COWBOY...
AND GO HOME WITH TH' ARMA-DILLOS...
TO SEE MY DEAR OL' MOTHER, WHOSE BACK'S AGAINST TH' WALL--
REDNECK!

AT THE END OF 1973, KENNETH LET HIS 40th CONSECUTIVE BEER LICENSE EXPIRE AND CLOSED THREADGILL'S.

YOU EITHER GOT TO EXPAND YOUR SEATING CAPACITY OR TURN PEOPLE AWAY.
I AIN'T GOT THE MONEY FOR THE FIRST, OR THE HEART FOR THE SECOND.

THE PLACE BARELY ESCAPED BEING DEMOLISHED BY THE CITY OF AUSTIN IN '74.
IT'S A HEALTH HAZARD AND AN EYESORE TO BOOT!
WAHL, I'D LIKE TO SEE THE BUILDING REMAIN FOR SENTIMENTAL REASONS.
CITY OF AUSTIN

BOARDED UP, THREADGILL'S SAT FORELORNLY ON NORTH LAMAR, BUT ITS MEMORY LIVED ON FOR THOSE WHO HAD KNOWN ITS BETTER DAYS.
Janis sang here

A COLLECTION OF KENNETH'S MUSIC WAS FINALLY RELEASED IN 1974 BY ROD KENNEDY, THE ORGANIZER OF THE KERRVILLE FOLK FESTIVAL. IT WAS CALLED YESTERDAY AND TODAY.
I LIKE THE YESTERDAYS BETTER THAN THE TODAYS...
THREADGILL

ONE WHO HAD NOT FORGOTTEN THREADGILL'S PLACE WAS EDDIE WILSON, NOW WEARY OF THE HECTIC SCENE AT AWHQ.
EDDIE, TH' KITCHEN STOVE...
EDDIE WE GOTTA COME UP WITH $5000 IN HALF AN HOUR, OR THAT OUTTA TOWN BAND WON'T GET ON THE STAGE.
EDDIE, TH' MEN'S TOILETS ARE STOPPED UP AGAIN AND IT'S FLOODING THE DANCE FLOOR!
MOAN...

IN 1976, HE QUIT AWHQ AND STARTED A HOLE-IN-THE-WALL RESTAURANT OFF 6th STREET CALLED THE RAW DEAL.

AFTER AWHILE, EDDIE BEGAN CASTING ABOUT FOR SOMEWHERE ELSE TO COOK.

OLD FRIENDS LIKE JOHNNY GIMBLE JOINED HIM FOR AN AUSTIN-PRODUCED ALBUM CALLED SILVER HAIRED DADDY.

THE RESTAURANT WAS AN INSTANT SUCCESS. TO HANDLE THE CROWDS, EDDIE ADDED A STAINLESS STEEL DINER ON THE SOUTH SIDE.

PRICELESS RELICS--LIKE A TEXAS-SHAPED NEON SHINER BEER SIGN--WERE LOST, BUT EDDIE WOULDN'T LET THE PLACE DIE.

SEEKING A LOAN TO REBUILD, EDDIE HAD A WEIRD FLASH OF DEJA VU WHEN HE WENT TO HIS BANK ON 9th AND CONGRESS...

KENNETH THREADGILL PASSED AWAY MAR. 20, 1987, LONG SINCE RECOGNIZED AS THE "DEAN OF THE AUSTIN MUSIC SCENE."

THOUGH KENNETH HAD STOPPED HIS WEDNESDAY NITE SESSIONS IN 1985, MUSICIANS LIKE JIMMIE DALE GILMORE RESUMED THEM IN '89 TO KEEP THE TRADITION ALIVE.

THAT YEAR KENNETH AND JANIS WERE HONORED BY THE CITY OF AUSTIN WITH STARS ON 6th STREET.

DURING THE FREEZE OF '84, BEULAH SPOTTED A PAN OF SPINACH CASSEROLE SITTING OUT BACK IN THE SNOW.

THAWED OUT, IT TASTED GOOD AS EVER.

SO WAS BORN THREADGILL'S LINE OF FROZEN VEGETABLES, THE FAVORITE SIDE DISHES THAT OUR CUSTOMERS CAN NEVER GET ENOUGH OF.

WHAT'S NEXT AT THREADGILL'S? WE CAN ONLY BE SURE THAT IT WILL INCLUDE GOOD FOOD, COLD BEER, AND AUSTIN MUSIC -- IN THE GRAND TRADITION THAT KENNETH THREADGILL STARTED BACK IN 1933. YES FOLKS, IT'S STILL JUST A NICE LITTLE FAMILY BUSINESS OUT ON NORTH LAMAR.

jaxon·94

THE SCRAPBOOK

Until we get modern enough to put a sound track and aromas in this scrapbook, just consider these visuals as hold'ja overs and appetizers for the memory.

THREADGILL'S: THE STATION (left) and the newlyweds (below). Mildred and Kenneth in the '30s...

...the 40's

...and the 50's

GARAGE BANDS AND GRUNGE have been around since practice made perfect. These were the kind of guys who ate pig's feet with their longnecks.

THE TEXAS TOP HANDS (Left) and Delores and the Bluebonnet Boys (Below) were just two of the bands that backed up Kenneth on his Al Jolsen and Jimmy Rodgers numbers.

THE WILSON FAMILY: Beulah, Woody and Eddie circa '50 (left) and '60 with Frank (below).

KENNETH AND THE GIRLS: Kay, Dottie and Becky (left to right) in the early '50s.

All Photos: Threadgill's Archives unless otherwise noted.

"JANIS CALLED ME DADDY." That's what Kenneth Threadgill recalled in this excerpt from the *Houston Chronicle* in August 1972:

"Janis first sang in public right here in the beer hall," Threadgill says. "It was about 10 years ago. It was funny how we met her. Julie Joyce—my drummer—saw her walking down 19th Street carrying an auto-harp. With her was Lannie Wiggins with his banjo on his back and Powell St. John toting a harmonica. They'd been playing for their own entertainment in the park."

Julie rapped with them and led them to Threadgill's bar for a refreshing beer and a chance to exhibit their musical form. They sometimes played before as many as 200 music lovers, including the college crowd, which jammed the place. Janis sang there for more than a year and was a loud, rowdy and vital force during Wednesday night jam sessions.

What did Threadgill think of her voice?

"It was high and shrill. That was my first impression. She sang Bluegrass and I guess I wasn't too impressed at first. But later she got real popular, singing folk music and rock, and could really punch and put over a song."

Mrs. Threadgill is itching to get in her say and finally does.

"Janis was a character. Cussed like a sailor and usually wore jeans and a coonskin cap. Wore it over the worst mess of hair your ever saw.

"One day she was sitting at the table and I came in with my Polaroid and told her to fix her hair and I'd take her picture. It was long and tangled—a mess. She didn't want to but then she combed it and I said put on some lipstick. She said she'd never had a lipstick in her whole borned days. But I talked her into it and when she saw herself in the mirror she said she wouldn't believe it was her if she didn't know it."

Says Threadgill: "Janis—she was a good ol' gal."

YOUNG JANIS JOPLIN and Mildred Threadgill at the Joint (above). On right, from top to bottom: Janis in her coonskin cap; Janis singing and picking with friends on a Wednesday night in '63; Kenneth and Mildred behind the bar in '72.

Photo: Houston Chronicle

Poster: JFKLN

Photo: © David Gahr

JANIS AND KENNETH circa 1970.

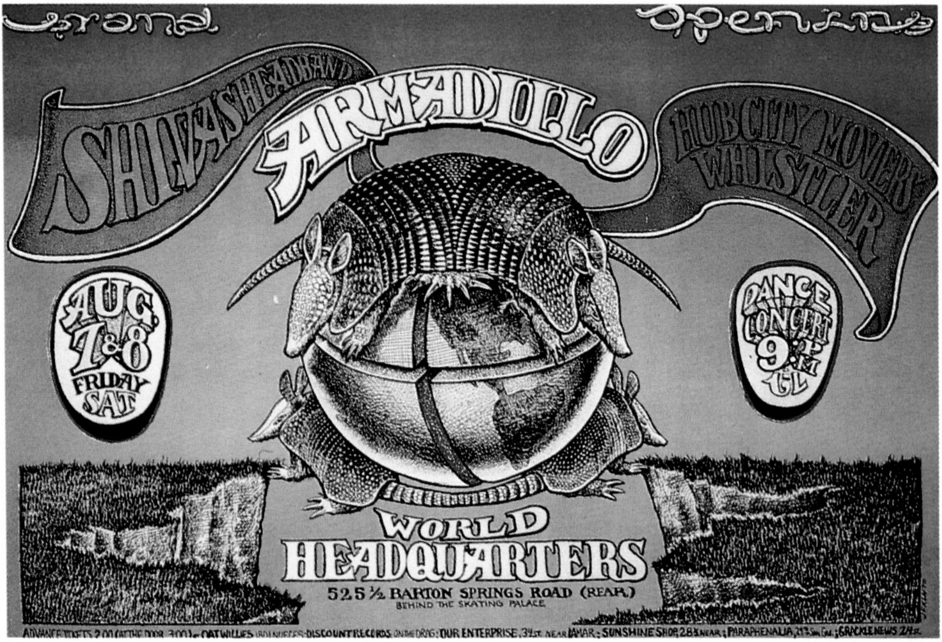

Poster: JFKLN

ARMADILLO WORLD HEADQUARTERS opened with music, art and daily bread.

ON THE FIRST HALOWEEN we had no pie, but we stomped a lot of pumpkins.

Poster: JFKLN

THE STRING BAND liked incredible spaghetti.

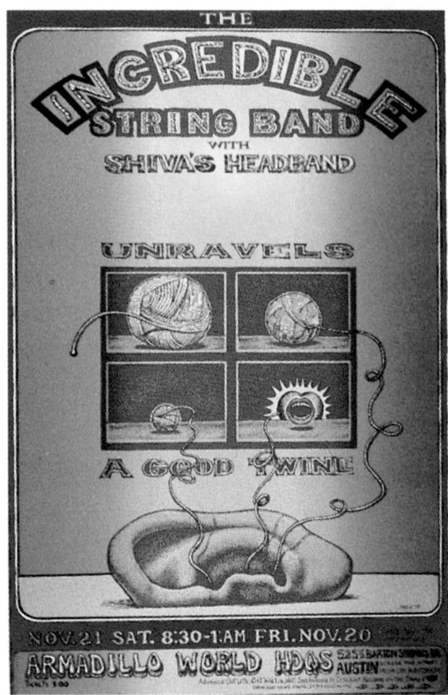

Poster: JFKLN

Photo: Burton Wilson

ON THE FIRST THANKSGIVING we had no turkeys. We had (left to right) Leon Russell, Mary Egan, Phil Lesh, Jerry Garcia, Doug Sahm and a host of others with no cover charge.

Photo: Burton Wilson

FATS DOMINO was nice, like red beans and rice.

Poster: JFKLN

THE FLYING BURRITO BROTHERS thought they had landed in hippie food heaven

BIG JOE WILLIAMS was one of the disciples of blues discovered by the local white kids of the '60s.

FRANK ZAPPA, ONE OF THE NICEST gentlemen that ever played Armadillo World Headquarters, was so impressed with the efforts by the Armadillo kitchen staff to serve good, wholesome food that he purchased a mixer and a pizza oven for us.

WILLIE NELSON altered Austin's consciousness about picnics and the 4th of July.

MANCE LIPSCOMB (left) broke the redneck color barrier in Austin by playing at Threadgill's in the '60s. When he was felled by a stroke in '74 we got Taj Mahal (right) to play a benefit performance at Armadillo. They flank Bill Neely, Kenneth's long-time musical sidekick.

All Photos this page by Burton Wilson

Poster: M. Preist

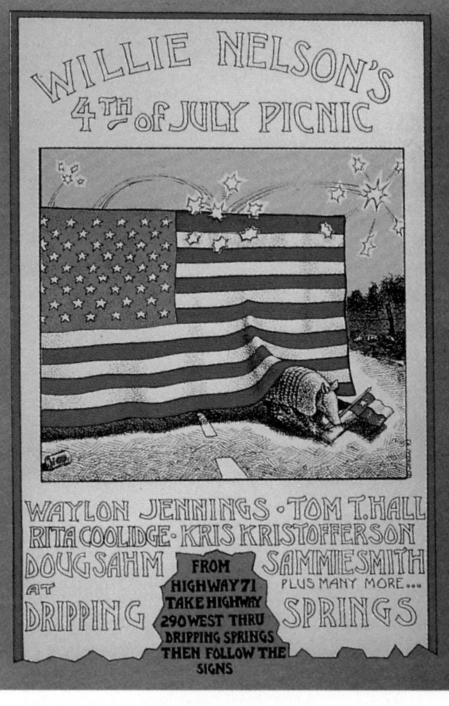

Poster: JFKLN

WILLIE'S FIRST ARMADILLO GIG was Michael Priest's first Armadillo poster (left). Willie's picnic (right and below) was no ordinary catering job.

Photo: Burton Wilson

Photo: Burton Wilson Mural: JFKLN

THE OPPOSITE of a visionary. I was an illusionary.

Photo: Burton Wilson

ARMADILLO WAS A convergence of people wanting to have jobs in a playhouse, working at a fantasy. Lifestyle was an accepted art form. We figured that if we worked hard enough and were good-hearted enough, somehow the rent would take care of itself.

BRUCE SPRINGSTEEN (right) was disappointed that we were out of shrimp enchiladas.

Photo: Coke Disworth

THE ARMADILLO STAFF inside and outside.

Photo: Coke Disworth

BIG RIKKE (below) could make a meal out of almost anyone.

Mural: JFKLN

IN THE BEER GARDEN with Greezy Wheels.

Poster: JFKLN

THE NIGHTS NEVER GET LONELY
by Gary P. Nunn and Bob Livingston
Publ. Rip Snortin' Tunes

Dancing in the moon light
under Lone Star skies
In a Lone Star state
With a Lone Star high
And the nights, they never get lonely.

We watch the showers of April
grow the flowers of May
We lay our cards on the table
Sing our songs all day
And the nights, they never get lonely.

Loving with your lover in the evening breeze
Listen to the murmur of the Spanish oak trees
Sweet soul music bring you to your knees
And the nights, they never get lonely.

Bean Taco and Harina tortilla
All night long
Bean Taco and Harina tortilla
Lone Star beer

AFTER MILDRED PASSED AWAY, Kenneth closed the tired old tavern and it sat vacant while he hit the road with the Hootenanny Hoots.

KENNETH HAD TWO CUTS on Willie's platinum soundtrack *Honeysuckle Rose*.

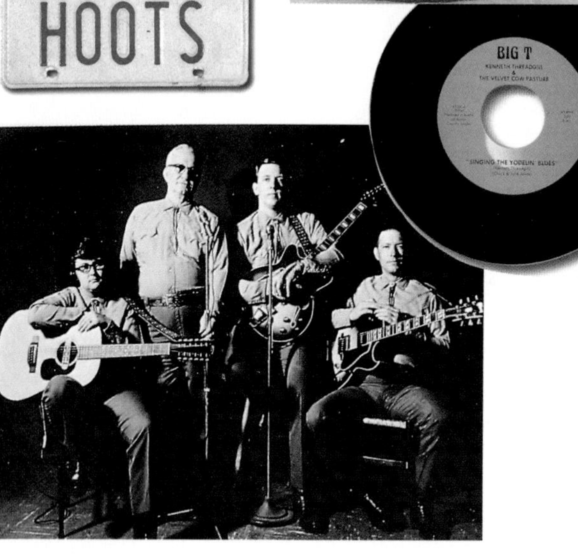

Poster: Ken Featherston

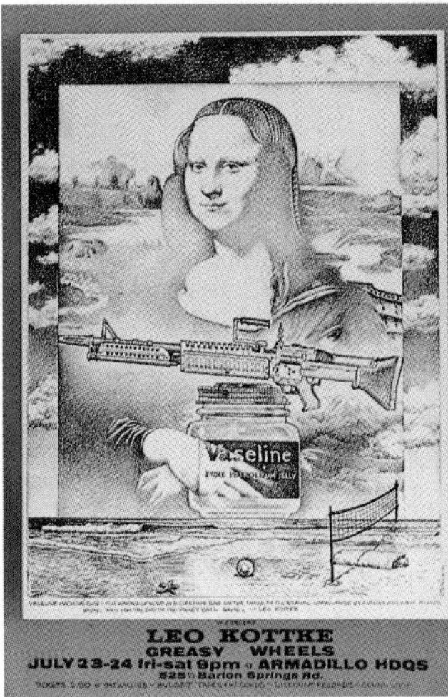

Poster: JFKLN

LEO KOTTKE AND GREEZY WHEELS at the Armadillo (above).

WE BEGAN TURNING Threadgills into a restaurant in 1979 (below).

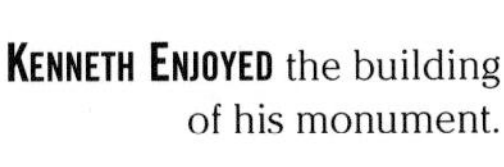
KENNETH ENJOYED the building of his monument.

Poster: M. Preist

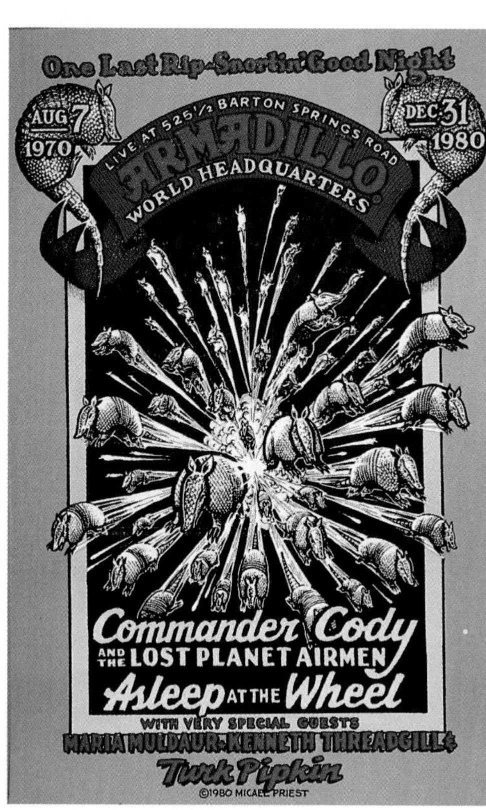

KENNETH PLAYED the last dance at the 'dillo.

Illustration: M. Preist

THE RAW DEAL, where the pork chop was king.

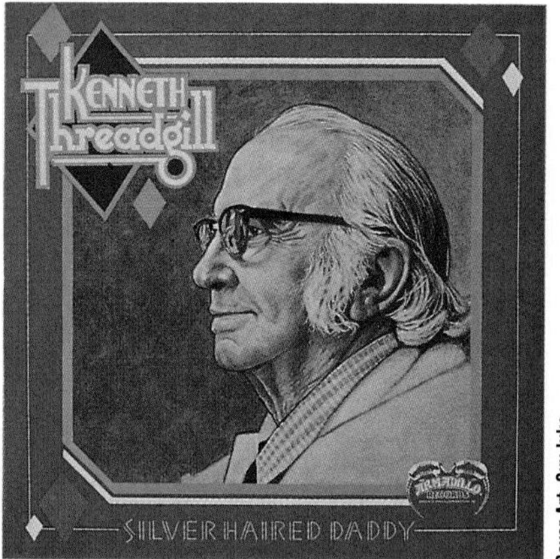

Cover Art: Guy Juke

SILVER HAIRED DADDY by Kennth Threadgill was the last album produced in the Armadillo's Onion Audio recording studio.

Poster: Bill Narum

WE OPENED THREADGILL'S with Bill Narum's CFS poster. We nailed up this poster promotion for chicken-fried steak all over central Texas.

THE JOINT THAT WON'T go out: August 16, 1982.

AFTER THE FIRE, Threadgill's became an "in tents" little joint.... We just kept on singing and rebuilt.

WITH THE HELP of Beulah and Woody, we added the commissary and the new joint was cooking again in 98 days!

JIMMIE DALE GILMORE and the Troubadours carry on Kenneth's tradition of Sittin', Singin' and Supper. Pictured here, left to right: Marvin Dykhuis, Dave Heath, Jimmie Dale Gilmore, Ron Erwin and Champ Hood.

THIS IS THE EVENT that got us christened the Carnegie Hall of Supper.

Poster: Kevin Combs

Photo: Scott Van Osdol

Poster: JFKLN

MOMMA FOUND the frozen spinach casserole in the snow of '84 (upper left).

WE STARTED taking Threadgill's to Texas grocery stores in 1991 (above).

IN '94 WE HAD A HOMECOMING (left) and 20,000 'dillos showed up.

"I wanna go home with the Armadillo.
Good country music from Amarillo to Abilene.
The friendliest people and the prettiest women you've ever seen."

"London Homesick Blues"
Gary P. Nunn

Photo: Burton Wilson

MOM AND POP for the millenium, Eddie and Sandra.

THE BOOK SEARCH
(FOR HIGH ADVENTURE)

I LOVE KITCHENS, AND I LOVE TO READ. I must love food more than books because I'm more plump than smart. Over the years, no matter what fine desk or spacious office might be available to me, I've found myself reading and writing at the kitchen table. I can read about food anywhere, and I can read about anything in the kitchen. Aunt Frances used to fuss at me for reading at the supper table. She said I didn't chew my food enough when I read and ate at the same time. She also said I wasn't supposed to talk with my mouth full. We didn't get along all that well, and we mostly saw each other at the supper table. The ability to enjoy fine dining is unique to the human species, but it seems that all animals can be grouchy when crowded around the trough.

Shopping for cooking or eating is a little like studying for finals. Sooner or later, it's gotta be done. The better you've shopped, the better the meal.

Prepping to cook is a bit like warming up before a workout. It is a time to move slowly, to get everything in its place, to think through what will follow, to visualize the end result.

Reading about food is a time to discover. It can be done between meals, or after you're too full for another bite.

Searching for books to read about food can be a grand adventure. I love old, dusty used bookstores, flea markets, garage sales, estate sales and libraries. My only gripe with libraries is they don't have beer and they make you whisper. As important as oral history is to piecing together our frontier past, it seems that our institutions are a bit out of balance. The lack of books in grog houses cause myths to grow to outsized proportions. When I stumble upon an important fact in a library, I want to shout for joy. Wrong place for joy, right place for facts.

Although I've spent a good bit of time in used bookstores, it wasn't until I discovered John Egerton's wonderful bibliography in *Southern Food* that I became disciplined in my pursuit to find more books that were fun about food. In fact, I was so impressed with Egerton's 32-page list that I reduced it to little bitty on a copy machine and carried it with me so that I would have it whenever I stumbled into a used bookstore.

Leah Chase had begun my Southern food education years ago with the comment that "the people in the Deep South do a lotta strange things with their grits." She was serving us a dish of shrimp in red gravy to be poured over grits. I was dumb as a freshman tackle and thought New Orleans was surely Deep South. No, Mrs. Chase assured me, Deep South meant Charleston. I realized I didn't know anything at all about what I loved most, Southern food.

Southern Food: At Home, on the Road, in History, by John Egerton with assistance from Ann Bleidt Egerton (University of North Carolina Press, Chapel Hill, 1993). The 1987 edition was awarded "Best Book on Food" laurels by the Culinary Institute of America. It is an inspiration. If you are interested in Southern food, you should not be without this book.

The Buster Holmes Restaurant Cookbook, New Orleans Handmade Cookin', by Buster Holmes (Pelican Publishing Co., Gretna, La., 1983). Buster's joint was an early inspiration for mine. Never has a restaurant felt so much like home to so many. This little book is the only omission from the Egerton bibliography of Southern food.

TEXAS

Since Egerton omitted Texas in his coverage of Southern food, I'll add a few of my favorite Texas recipe references to my recommendation that you acquire his bibliography if you have a serious interest in Southern cooking.

Cuisine, Texas: A Multiethnic Feast, by Joanne Smith (University of Texas Press, Austin, 1995). Makes you proud to be a Texan of at least two dozen different origins.

Cooking Texas Style, by Candy Wagner and Sandra Marquez (University of Texas Press, Austin, 1993). Wonderfully useful, simple, practical.

Texas Home Cooking, by Cheryl Alters Jamison and Bill Jamison (Harvard Common Press, Boston, 1993). A first-class piece of work—even if they did change the name of our Creole Cabbage.

***Texas Highways* Cookbook**, by Joanne Smith (University of Texas Press, Austin, 1986). *Texas Highways* magazine and this wonderful cookbook give us a reason to be proud of our state government.

The Texas Cookbook, by Mary Faulk Koock (Little, Brown and Co., Boston, 1965). They don't get much better than this.

The San Antonio Cookbook, collected by The Women's Committee of the San Antonio Symphony Society, 1962.

Best of the Best from Texas: Selected Recipes from Texas' Favorite Cookbooks, ed. by Gwen McKee and Barbara Moseley (Quail Ridge Press, Brandon, Miss., 1985).

READING FOR FLAVOR

It is sometimes restful to read about food without planning to cook. These books are not all even about food. They are about flavor.

Food for Thought: An Anthology of Writings Inspired by Food, ed. by Joan and John Digby (William Morrow and Co., New York, 1987). Not as funny as Roy Blount, but we've got to have other books to read while we wait for Roy to write another.

Mrs. Rasmussen's Book of One-Arm Cookery with Second Helpings, by Mary Lasswell (Houghton Mifflin Co., Boston, 1970). An update of the 1945 edition in which the author teaches recipes that can be accomplished with one hand, leaving the other free to handle a glass of cold beer. Very good style and excellent recipes.

Oral Sadism and the Vegetarian Personality: Readings from the Journal of Polymorphous Perversity, ed. by Glenn C. Ellenbogen, Ph.D. (Ballantine Books, New York, 1986). For 10 cents at a garage sale, you can sometimes make yourself feel like a wise investor.

Gumbo Ya-Ya: Folk Tales of Louisiana, by Lyle Saxon (Pelican Publishing Co., Gretna, La., 1987). A great book for picking up Louisiana flavors in more than just food.

Junk Food, by Rubin, Rollert, Farago, Stark and Etra (Dell, New York 1980). Seldom does a book do such justice to its name.

HISTORY

This section could be combined easily with the Collector's section since some of the best reading on the subject is out of print.

Pease Porridge Hot: Recipes, Household Hints & Home Remedies of the Pease Family, annotated by Katherine Hart (a Waterloo Book published by the Encino Press for the Friends of the Austin Public Library, 1967). The selected letters of the Pease family show that in the mid-1800s, the three most common problems were mud, health care and food supplies.

Notes on the Republic, by Ellen N. Murry (Star of the Republic Museum, Washington, Tex., 1991). First-class work, Ms. Murry. I hope to meet you someday. The chapters on food and grog houses are indispensable.

Indian Givers, by Jack Weatherford (a Fawcett Columbine book published by Ballantine Books, New York, 1988). My favorite American history book. It puts a lot more than our food sources into perspective.

American Diner: Then and Now, by Richard J. S. Gutman (Harper

Perennial, New York, 1993) and **The American Drive-In,** by Michael Karl Witzel (Motorbooks Int'l Pubs. & Wholesalers, Osceola, Wisc., 1994). From horse-drawn lunch counters to the automobile, these books give depth and the ideas of picture books.

American Food: The Gastronomic Story, Including a Personal Treasury of More Than 500 Distinctive Regional, Traditional and Contemporary Recipes, by Evan Jones (E.P. Dutton & Co., New York, 1975). This is where I learned that succotash was an American frozen food in the 1600s.

America's First Cuisines, by Sophie D. Coe (University of Texas Press, Austin, 1994). Talk about going way back.

COLLECTOR TIPS

Cookbooks Worth Collecting, by Mary Barile (Wallace-Homestead Book Co., 1994). A helpful starter guide with a good history and good collector sources.

H.T. Hicks Collector's Guide to Old Cookbooks, by H.T. and J.M. Hicks. This book is a pricing guide for the advanced collector.

A Guide to Collecting Cookbooks, by Colonel Bob Allen (Collector Books, 1990). Includes a large price guide and lots of color illustrations of collectable cookbooks.

The Lily Wallace New American Cook Book, edited by Lily Haxworth Wallace (Books, Inc., New York, 1949).

Household Discoveries by Sidney Morse & Mrs. Curtis's Cook Book, by Isabel Gordon Curtis (Success Company's Branch Offices, Petersburg, N.Y.; Toledo, Ohio; Danville, Ill.; Oklahoma City, Okla.; San Jose, Cal., 1914). I found it in a trash pile and I wouldn't take a buncha bucks for it!

Favorite Recipes of Famous Women, with a foreword by Florence Stratton (Harper & Brothers, Publishers, New York and London, 1925). This breakfast recipe, from Mrs. F. Scott Fitzgerald, is just one good example of what entertainment can be found in secondhand bookstores for pennies: "See if there is any bacon, and if there is ask the cook which pan to fry it in. Then ask if there are any eggs, and if so try and persuade the cook to poach two of them. It is better not to attempt toast, as it burns very easily. Also in the case of bacon do not turn the fire too high, or you will have to get out of the house for a week. Serve preferably on china plates, though gold or wood will do if handy."

Feeding the Family, by Mary Swartz Rose, Ph.D. (Macmillan Co., New York, 1917). This is the way to study history instead of studying *about* history.

Culinary Arts Institute Encyclopedic Cookbook, ed. by Ruth Berolzheimer (Culinary Arts Institute, Chicago, 1950 and 1973). By having several editions of cookbooks reissued over many years, you get a very clear picture of what comes and what goes.

The Cook Book by "Oscar" of the Waldorf, by Oscar Tschirky, Maitre d' Hotel, The Waldorf (The Werner Co., Chicago, New York, 1896). This is a treasure when found in good condition. Mine is ragged, but it is autographed by Oscar and cost me a dollar. That's only about 25 cents a pound.

SPECIALTY

A kitchen reference library is easy to build cheaply. Manufacturers of many sorts put out good, inexpensive books to teach you every possible way to use their products. Kerr Glass Corporation and Ball Home Canning Products are great examples. Their books are encyclopedic guides and cost about four dollars new. The Storey Publishing Bulletins cost about three dollars and cover dozens of food topics as thoroughly as culinary school textbooks. From wine and beer to bread and cheese, and many more, are in easy reach for less effort and money than some trips to the library.

Frequently you find one book that covers many versions of the same subject. Sandra's garden keeps her looking for methods of dealing with problems ranging from bounty to bugs. Her books rest comfortably with our cookbooks, three for four steps from the kitchen table.

The following are a few of our current favorites:

The Ultimate Barbecue Sauce Cookbook, by Jim Auchmutey and Susan Puckett (Longstreet Press, Inc., Atlanta, 1995). If you have any doubts about what barbecue sauce means in any given part of the country, get this book. If you don't think you have any doubts, get it anyway.

A Consumer's Dictionary of Food Additives, by Ruth Winter, M.S. (Crown Publishers, New York, 1989). Once you start reading labels closely you've got to have a dictionary.

Nutrition Almanac, Third Edition, by Lavon J. Dunne (McGraw-Hill, 1990). This is the best basic guide to the subject I've found. Thousands of everyday foods can be looked up in a jiffy.

Jay Harlow's Beer Cuisine: A Cookbook for Beer Lovers, by Jay Harlow (an Astolat Book published by Harlow & Ratner, Emeryville, Calif., 1991).

Peppers: The Domesticated Capsicums, written and illustrated by Jean Andrews (University of Texas Press, Austin, 1984). The ultimate marriage of art and food and the reason for a coffee table.

Stocking Up: The Third Edition of the Classic Preserving Guide, by Carol Hupping and the staff of the Rodale Food Center (a Fireside Book published by Simon & Schuster, 1986).

The Sausage-Making Cookbook, by Jerry Predika (Stackpole Books,

1983). A lot more appetizing than watching the Texas legislature pass laws, this tidy little book takes the grim mystery out of sausages of all sorts.

Preserving Summer's Bounty: A Quick and Easy Guide to Freezing, Canning, Preserving and Drying What You Grow, ed. by Susan McClure and the Staff of the Rodale Food Center (Rodale Press, Emmaus, Pa., 1995). If you're going to the effort to put in a garden, you should have this book for the day when you just can't eat it all.

Fresh from the Garden: Time Honored Recipes from the Readers of *Texas Gardener*, ed. by Rita Miller (TG Press, 1986).

Cooking Wild Game and Fish Mississippi Style, by Billy Joe Cross. (Probably a vanity press edition—no publisher or copyright—find your own, I love mine.)

Cooking with Pearl Beer, Pearl Brewing Co., San Antonio, and St. Joseph, Mo. (published by the Brewery as a promotion, probably about 1968). Made up of recipes contributed by distributors and their wives, this book proves that beer can always be substituted for water and improve any dish. Another good example of what Texans really ate during that period.

Ben & Jerry's Homemade Ice Cream & Dessert Book, by Ben Cohen and Jerry Greenfield with Nancy J. Stevens (Workman Publishing, New York, 1987). Bless their souls, these guys share my belief that secrets are for sharing. Spread the ease of goodness!

REDEDICATION

THINKING BACK on Mother and Mr. Threadgill, I realize how similar they were in several ways. Both had unusually wide streaks of tolerance and they were about the least aloof of any two folks I've ever known. They simply had not one iota of snobbishness in their souls. I never heard either one say, "I told you so."

They both seemed to genuinely care for every person they met without the slightest regard for how that person looked or what he had in his wallet. Wilson's Day Nursery School and Threadgill's were both just around the corner from what used to be called the Texas State Lunatic Asylum. Mother and Mr. Threadgill both saw an uncommon number of society's rejects and yet they acted like they couldn't tell an idiot from a preacher or a politician.

They both were enormously grateful for all they had. They said "thank you" an awful lot but never asked for much of anything so they didn't need to use "please" all that often. They were very confident of their strengths and used those strengths tirelessly to provide for their families. They were encouraging without giving all that much advice. Mother challenged me with, "You can do anything you set your mind to!"

Beulah was a genius with sick infants. Physicians whose children were enrolled in Wilson's Day Nursery looked to her for prognoses and recommendations of treatments for their own children when they were ill. Otherwise, I never heard her give much advice except to eat my vegetables. She would remind me to say my prayers, of course, and, God bless the memory, every time we parted she admonished me to "have fun!"

I knew Kenneth from the time he was about my age now until he reached over 80 years. He regretted that he waited so long to pursue his dream of a singing career, but he did what he had to do and enjoyed it to the fullest. He was the first "old guy" outside of the public school system who remembered me when I was a kid. He greeted me like I was an adult he was glad to see, and said, "Come back to see me," when I left his little old joint after a visit. And he really meant it, I could tell.

I have tried to follow Mother's advice. I eat my vegetables, say my prayers and have set my mind to have fun. I've also tried to follow the advice of Kenneth and his father, the Reverend John Threadgill: "Enjoy whatever you have to do and stay out of jail."

Now that the therapy for my bashfulness is working so well, I think I'll take singing lessons and maybe produce a television show that teaches kids to cook good food and play music. We'll start with a bacon and lettuce and homegrown tomato sandwich and a side of grits.

— *Eddie Wilson*

Index

Adams, Glenn Bob 22, 112, 154

Aiken, Harry 33

Alexander, Stan 11

Ambrosia 70

Amerindians 28
  Narragansett Indians 89–90

Apple Pie 159–60

Armadillo World Headquarters ix, 6, 12–15, 132, 174, 177
  Nachos 182–83

Auchmutey, Jim: *The Ultimate Barbecue Sauce Cookbook* 45

Aunt Onie 91

Aunt Onie's White Soda Cornbread 74–75

Austin, Texas ix, 15

Austin American-Statesman 167–68

Austin High School 178

Austin music scene 11–15

Austin Musicians' Appreciation Supper 14

Baked Beans 92–93

Baker, LaVerne 176

Baker Junior High 153

Banana Pudding 17, 156–57

Barton Springs Road 12

BBQ 113–14
  BBQ Rub 40
  BBQ Sauce 45–46

Beans
  Baked Beans 92–93
  Black Bean Soup 62
  Drunken Bean Soup 60
  Green Bean Salad 68
  Green Beans 93–94
  Old South Butter Beans 94
  Red Beans and Rice 95–96
  Refried Beans 97, 171, 183
  Santa Fe Succotash 89–90
  Texas Chili Beans 96

Beef
  Beef Liver with Onions 126–27
  Beef Stew 139
  Beef Stock 33, 34
  Bronzed Sirloin Pasta Salad 129
  Bronzed Sirloin Steak 127
  Chicken-fried Steak 116–17
  Chicken-fried Strips 185–86
  Hot Roast Beef Sandwich 151
  Meatloaf 130
  Pot Roast 139–40
  Steaks 142–43
  Beer: various brands and breweries 178–80

Ben & Jerry's ice cream 153

Big Brother and the Holding Company 12

Birdseye, Clarence 9

Biscuits
  Buttermilk Biscuits 76–77
  Threadgill's Biscuit Mix 76

Black Bean Soup 62

Black-eyed Peas 90
  Hopping John 91

Bloody Marys 168, 181

Blount, Roy, Jr. 2, 139
  "Health Food Blues" 56
  "Hymn to Ham" 150
  "Song to Bacon" 173
  "Song to Barbecue Sauce" 46
  "Song to Eggs" 188
  "Song to Grits" 103
  "Song to Okra" 106

B.L.T. (sandwich) 149

Blue Cheese Dressing 42–43

"Blue Yodeler, The" (Jimmie Rodgers) 9

Boiled Greens 98

Bon Appétit magazine 15

Branch, Janet x

Breads 71–79
  Aunt Onie's White Soda Cornbread 74–75
  Buttermilk Biscuits 76–77
  Cornbread Dressing 75–76
  Homestyle White Bread 78–79
  Jalapeño Corn Muffins 73–74
  Southern Cornbread 73
  Threadgill's Biscuit Mix 76
  Whole Wheat Bread 79
  Yeast Rolls 77–78

Breakfast 168–73

Breakfast Tacos 171–72

Broccoli 20, 98–99
  Broccoli and Rice Casserole 108–9
  Broccoli/Cauliflower Salad 65
  Cream of Broccoli Soup 58

Bronzed Catfish 127

Bronzed Sirloin Pasta Salad 129

Bronzed Sirloin Steak 127

Brown Gravy 53, 151

Brunswick stew 18
Buffet, Jimmy 181
Butchers 26, 32–33
Butter 19, 71–72
Butter, Citrus 49
Butter Beans, Old South 94
Butter versus lard 19
Buttered Carrots 101
Buttermilk Biscuits 76–77
Buttermilk Pie 160–61

Cabbage 99–100
  Creole Cabbage 99, 100, 107
Cajun-Italian Eggplant 105, 107
Cakes
  Mississippi Mud Cake 158
  Strawberry Shortcake 163–64
Callahan's General Store 153
Candied Sweet Potatoes 87
Carrots 83, 100–101
  Buttered Carrots 101
  Carrot and Raisin Salad 65
Casseroles 108–13
  Broccoli and Rice 108
  Macaroni and Cheese 111
  San Antonio Squash 109
  Spinach Casserole 110
  Spinach Casserole Bill Arnold 110–11
  Vegetarian Jambalaya 112
Cast-iron skillet 23
Castro, Sam 168
Catfish 19
  Bronzed Catfish 127
  Catfish Moutarde 120
  French Quarter Catfish 133
  Fried Catfish 118
Caviar, Texas 68–69
Celery 88
Central Market. *See* H-E-B Central Market
Cherry Cola Jell-O™ 70
Chicken
  Bronzed Chicken Breast 127
  Chicken and Dumplings 138
  Chicken Enchiladas 136–37
  Chicken Pastalaya 125
  Chicken Salad Sandwich 151
  Chicken Stock 33, 34–35
  Chicken-fried Chicken Breasts and Cream Gravy 116–17
  Chicken-fried Strips 185–86
  Fried Chicken 117–18
  Fried Chicken Livers 19, 186
  Smoked Chicken Pasta Salad 128
Chicken-fried Pork Chops and Cream Gravy 116–17
Chicken-fried Steak and Cream Gravy 116–17
Chile con Queso 185
Chili
  Texas Chili Beans 96
  Texas Red Chili 140–41
Chili pequins (peppers) 20–21
Chipotle Cream Sauce 47
Chocolate
  Chocolate Brandy Cream 162
  Chocolate Chip Cookies 165
  Double Chocolate Ice Box Pie 161
Citrus Butter 49
Clark, Guy 2, 139
  "Homegrown Tomatoes" 27
  "Watermelon Dream" 148
Cliff, Jimmy 13
Cobbler, Peach 159
Cocktail Sauce 48
Cold Tomatillo Soup 62–63
Coleslaw 66
Combs, Kevin 2
"Comfort food" 17
  Macaroni and Cheese as 111
Convenience foods 26, 28–29
Cookies, Chocolate Chip 165
Corn
  Corn Soup 59–60
  Creamed Corn Diablo 102
  Roasting Ears 101
  Santa Fe Succotash 89–90
  Smoked Corn Relish 50–51
  Snap Peas, Peppers and Corn 97
  Sweet Corn off the Cob 74, 102
Cornbread 71
  Aunt Onie's White Soda Cornbread 74–75
  Cornbread Dressing 75–76
  Jalapeño Corn Muffins 73–74
  Southern Cornbread 73
Corps of Engineers, U.S. 9
Cottage Cheese and Cucumber Salad 66–67
Coyote Cafe 90
Cream, Whipped 164–65
Cream Gravy 51–52
Cream of Broccoli Soup 58
Creamed Corn Diablo 102

Creole Cabbage 99, 100, 107
Creole Sauce 46–47
Crowley, Mike x
Cucumber, Cottage Cheese and, Salad 66–67
Culinary Arts Institute 99

Daniels, Charlie 132
Davis, Jack 1
Delmonico Potatoes 83
Desserts 153–68
Double Chocolate Ice Box Pie 161
Dressings
  Blue Cheese Dressing 42–43
  Cornbread Dressing 75–76
  Hot Bacon Dressing for Spinach Salad 43
  Jalapeño Honey Mustard 43–44
  Lemon (or Lime) Mayonnaise 41–42
  Mayonnaise 41
  Thousand Island 44
  Vinegar and Oil 44
Dreyer's Grand Ice Cream 153
Drunken Bean Soup 60

Egerton, John 19, 20
Eggplant 104–5
Eggs
  Eggs Florentine 173
  Migas 171
  Spinach Omelets 172–73
Eli the Tailor 55
Ephron, Nora 167–68
Epicurean, The (Charles Ranhofer) 83

Farmer, Fanny 83
Fearing, Dean xi
Fig Preserves 170
Food and Drug Administration 55
Food Guide Pyramid (USDA) 19, 55, 82–83, 168, 176
Franklin, Jim 12–13
French Quarter Catfish 133
French Quarter Pasta Salad 67
Fresh Peas 92
Fried Catfish 118
Fried Chicken 117–18
Fried Chicken Livers 19, 176, 186
Fried Green Tomatoes 184–85
Fried Oysters 19, 119, 176
Frito Corn Chips 176
  in salad 63–64

Garlic 88
Garlic Cheese Grits 104
Gilmore, Jimmie Dale x, 11–12, 14
Glazed Ham with Jezebel Sauce 131
God Nose (Jack Jackson) 2
Gourmet magazine 15
Graham, Mike 55
Grandfather of Austin Country Music (Kenneth Threadgill) 3
Gravies 51–53
  Brown Gravy 53, 151
  Cream Gravy 51–52
  Skillet Cream Gravy 52–53
  Turkey Gravy 51
Great Depression 25, 26, 31, 99, 143
Green Bean Salad 68
Green Beans 93–94
Greens
  Boiled Greens 98
  Mustard Greens 64
Grillades and Grits 121
Grilled Ham and Cheese (sandwich) 150
Grits
  Garlic Cheese Grits 104
  Grillades and Grits 121
  "Song to Grits" (Roy Blount, Jr.) 103
Guinea melon or squash 104–5
Gumbo, Mumbo- 141–42

Haight-Ashbury (San Francisco) 6, 11
Ham 144
  Glazed Ham with Jezebel Sauce 131
  Grilled Ham and Cheese (sandwich) 150
  "Hymn to Ham" (Roy Blount, Jr.) 150
"Health Food Blues" (Roy Blount, Jr.) 56
Heartburn (movie) 168
H-E-B Central Market 26, 101
Herndon, John 177–78
Hightone Records x
History: of Threadgill's 9–15
Hold'ja Overs 174–88
Holy Trinity of Southern Cooking 88
"Homegrown Tomatoes" (Guy Clark) 27
Homestyle White Bread 78–79
Hood, Champ x

Hootenanny Hoots 11, 12
Hopping John 91
Horne, Lena 176
Horseradish Sour Cream Sauce 50
Hot Bacon Dressing for Spinach Salad 43
Hot Roast Beef Sandwich 151
Household Discoveries and Mrs. Curtis's Cook Book 23, 83, 99, 143–44
"Howdy Hour" 174
Hurt, William 167
"Hymn to Ham" (Roy Blount, Jr.) 150

Ice Cream, Vanilla 166

Jackson, Jack 2
Jalapeño Corn Muffins 73–74
Jalapeño Honey Mustard Dressing 43–44
Jalapeños, Stuffed 187
Jambalaya, Seafood 133–34
Jambalaya, Tenderloin 123
Jambalaya, Vegetarian 112–13
Jezebel Sauce 48
John Van Range Company (catalog) 23
Joplin, Janis 2, 3, 6, 7, 11, 12, 13, 15, 176

Kreutz Market 45–46
Kristofferson, Kris 13, 181

Lamar Street ix–x
Lard versus butter 19
Leary, Timothy 11
Lemon Mayonnaise 41–42
Lime Mayonnaise 41–42
Lipscomb, Mance 11
Liver
  Beef Liver with Onions 126–27
  Fried Chicken Livers 19, 176, 186
Lobster Taco xi
Loew's Theatre 10
"Low fat" foods 55–56, 188
Lumberton, Mississippi 9, 18, 25, 74

Macaroni and Cheese 19, 111
MacDowell, Andie 167
McCallum High School 10
McFarland, T. J. ix
Mansion on Turtle Creek Cookbook (Dean Fearing) xi
Margaritas 181–82
Mashed Potatoes 84
Mayonnaise 40, 41
  Lemon (or Lime) Mayonnaise 41–42
"Meat and three" 19, 22, 88
Meat Seasoning 38
Meatloaf 114–15, 130
  Nashville Meatloaf 131–32
Michael (movie) 167–68
Microwave ovens 23, 24
Midler, Bette 13
Migas 171
Miller, Mark 23, 90
Miracle Whip 64
Mississippi, southern 17
Mississippi Mud Cake 158
Mock Hash Brown Potatoes 172
Monterey Pop Festival 12
Morrison, Van 13
Mother's (restaurant) 99, 144, 146–47
Mrs. Curtis's Cook Book, Household Discoveries and 23, 83, 99, 143–44
Mumbo–Gumbo 141–42
Murry, Ellen: *Notes on the Republic* 177
Mushroom Caps, Stuffed 187

Nachos, Armadillo World Headquarters 182–83
Naragansett Indians 89–90
Nashville, Tennessee 13
Nashville Meatloaf 131–32
National Geographic 14
Nations, Carrie 177
Neely, Bill ix
Nelson, Willie 9, 13, 15, 147, 181
New Potatoes with Garlic and Green Beans 85
Newport Folk Festival 12
Newsweek 14
Night Hawk Restaurant 33
North Austin, Texas 11
Notes on the Republic (Ellen Murry) 177

Okra 106–7
  Pickled Okra 106

"Song to Okra" (Roy Blount, Jr.) 106
Stewed Okra and Tomatoes 107

Old South Butter Beans 94

Olestra 55, 188

Omelets, Spinach 172

Onions 88

Oysters
Fried Oysters 19, 119, 176
Spinach and Oyster Pie 134–35

Pasta
French Quarter Pasta Salad 67
Macaroni and Cheese 111
Smoked Chicken Pasta Salad 128

Pastalaya 124
Chicken Pastalaya 125
Pastalaya Base 48–49
Seafood Pastalaya 124
Vegetable Pastalaya 125–26

Peach Cobbler 159

Pearl (Janis Joplin recording) 12

Peas 89, 90–92
Black-eyed Peas 90
Fresh Peas 92
Hopping John 91
Peas and carrots 100
Santa Fe Succotash 89–90
Snap Peas, Peppers and Corn 97
Texas Caviar 68–69

Pecan Delight Pie (Salty Cracker Pie) 157

Pecan Pie 155–56

Pecan trees 25

Picnics 144–47

Pies
Apple Pie 159–60
Buttermilk Pie 160–61
Double Chocolate Ice Box Pie 161
Peach Cobbler 159
Pecan Delight Pie (Salty Cracker Pie) 157
Pecan Pie 155–56
Pie Crust 155
Pumpkin Pie 162–63
Salty Cracker Pie 157
Spinach and Oyster Pie 134–35
Strawberry-Rhubarb Pie 166–67
Sweet Potato Honey Pie 164

Pig Stand (drive-in) 143

Poboys (sandwiches) 99, 146

Polson, Roger x

Poplarville, Mississippi 74

Pork 143–44
Chicken-fried Pork Chops and Cream Gravy 116–17
Grillades and Grits 121
Grilled Ham and Cheese (sandwich) 150
Ham 144
Glazed Ham with Jezebel Sauce 131
Grilled Ham and Cheese (sandwich) 150
"Hymn to Ham" (Roy Blount, Jr.) 150
Split Pea and Ham Soup 60–61
Pork Stroganoff 122
Smothered Pork Chops 132
Southwest Pork Chops 128
Tenderloin Jambalaya 123

Potatoes. *See also* Sweet Potatoes
Mashed Potatoes 84
Mock Hash Brown Potatoes 172
New Potatoes with Garlic and Green Beans 85
Potato Salad 69
Scalloped Potatoes 86

Pot foods 137–42

Pot Roast 139–40

Poultry. *See* Chicken

Preserves, Fig 170

Presley, Elvis 63

Puckett, Susan: *The Ultimate Barbecue Sauce Cookbook* 45

Pudding, Banana 17, 156–57

Pumpkin Pie 162–63

Ranhofer, Charles: *The Epicurean* 83

Raw Deal 2, 13, 14

Red Beans and Rice 95–96

Reed, John ix

Refried Beans 97, 171, 183

Relish, Smoked Corn 50–51

Rice
Broccoli and Rice Casserole 108–9
Hopping John 91
Red Beans and Rice 95–96

Richards, Ann 9, 14, 15

Roasting Ears (corn) 101

Rodgers, Jimmie 9–10

Rolling Stone 14

Sabine Street 13

Salads 63–70
Ambrosia 70
Broccoli/Cauliflower Salad 65

Bronzed Sirloin Pasta Salad 129
Carrot and Raisin Salad 65
Cherry Cola Jell-O™ 70
Coleslaw 66
Cottage Cheese and Cucumber Salad 66–67
French Quarter Pasta Salad 67
Green Bean Salad 68
Potato Salad 69
Smoked Chicken Pasta Salad 128
Texas Caviar 68–69

Salsa Verde 137

Salt and salt substitutes 20

Salty Cracker Pie 157

San Antonio Squash Casserole 109

San Francisco, California 6, 11

Sandwiches 144–51
B.L.T. 149
Chicken Salad Sandwich 151
Grilled Ham and Cheese 150
Hot Roast Beef Sandwich 151

Santa Fe Succotash 89–90

Sauces 45–53
BBQ Sauce 45
Brown Gravy 53, 151
Chipotle Cream Sauce 47
Citrus Butter 49
Cocktail Sauce 48
Cream Gravy 51–52
Creole Sauce 46–47
Horseradish Sour Cream Sauce 50
Jezebel Sauce 48
Pastalaya Base 48–49
Salsa Verde 137
Skillet Cream Gravy 52–53
Smoked Corn Relish 50–51
Tartar Sauce 50
Turkey Gravy 51

Scalloped Potatoes 86

Schmidt, Rick 45–46

Seafood
Seafood Jambalaya 133–34
Seafood Pastalaya 124
Seafood Seasoning 39

Seasonings 37–40
BBQ Rub 40
Meat Seasoning 38
Poultry Seasoning 38
Seafood Seasoning 39
Vegetable Seasoning 39

Sheraton, Mimi 19

Sheridan, Francis 177

Shiva's Headband 12

Simpson, Scooter 57

Sittin', Singin' and Supper Sessions x, 2, 10, 14

Skating Palace 12

Skillet Cream Gravy 52–53

Smith, Bessie 176

Smithsonian 14

Smoked Chicken Pasta Salad 128

Smoked Corn Relish 50–51

Smothered Pork Chops 132

Snap Peas, Peppers and Corn 97

Somewhere Stand, The (burger stand) 63

"Song to Bacon" (Roy Blount, Jr.) 173

"Song to Barbecue Sauce" (Roy Blount, Jr.) 46

"Song to Eggs" (Roy Blount, Jr.) 188

"Song to Grits" (Roy Blount, Jr.) 103

"Song to Okra" (Roy Blount, Jr.) 106

Soups 57–63
Black Bean Soup 62
Cold Tomatillo Soup 62
Corn Soup 59–60
Cream of Broccoli Soup 58
Drunken Bean Soup 60
Split Pea and Ham Soup 60–61
Tomato Soup 59
Tortilla Soup 61
Vegetable Soup 58–59

Sour Cream Sauce, Horseradish 50

Southern Cornbread 73

Southern Spices 37

Southwest Pork Chops 128

Spinach
Eggs Florentine 173
Spinach and Oyster Pie 134–35
Spinach Casserole 110
Spinach Casserole Bill Arnold 110–11
Spinach Omelets 172
Spinach Pizza 136

Split Pea and Ham Soup 60–61

Split Rail 11

Springsteen, Bruce 13

Square One (dining room) 7

Squash
San Antonio Squash Casserole 109
Yellow Squash 107–8

Steak 142–43
Bronzed Sirloin Pasta Salad 129
Bronzed Sirloin Steak 127
Chicken-fried Steak 116–17

Stewed Okra and Tomatoes 107

Stocks 32–36
  Beef Stock 33, 34
  Chicken Stock 34–35
  Turkey Stock 35
  Vegetable Stock 33, 36
Strawberry-Rhubarb Pie 166–67
Strawberry Shortcake 163–64
Streusel Topping 159–60
Stroganoff, Pork 122
Stuffed Jalapeños 187
Stuffed Mushroom Caps 187
Stuffed Trout 135
Swanson, Roger 64, 98
Sweet Corn off the Cob 74, 102
Sweet Potatoes
  Candied Sweet Potatoes 87
  Sweet Potato Honey Pie 164
  Yams or Sweet Potatoes, Baked or Mashed 86–87
"Sweet tea" 20

Tabasco Sauce 63
Taj Mahal 13
Tartar Sauce 50
Teflon 23, 25
Temperance Society 178
Tenderloin Jambalaya 123
Texas beers 178–80
Texas Caviar 68–69
Texas Chili Beans 96
Texas Home Cooking 99
Texas Red Chili 140–41
Threadgill, Becky 57
Threadgill, Dottie 10–11
Threadgill, Kay 57
Threadgill, Kenneth ix, x, 3, passim
Threadgill, Mildred 11, 13
Threadgill, Reverend John 237
Threadgill's
  Commissary 3, 6, 14
  Country Store Museum and Banquet Hall 6, 14
  Frozen Food 14–15, 28
  "The Upstairs Store" 3, 6, 14, 19, passim
Threadgill's Biscuit Mix 76
Thousand Island Dressing 44
Three-Salad Lunch Special 69
Tomato Soup 59
Tomatoes, Fried Green 184–85
Tortilla Soup 61
Travolta, John 167
Trout, Stuffed 135
Tucker, Ned 63
Turkey
  Turkey Gravy 51
  Turkey Stock 35

Ultimate Barbecue Sauce Cookbook (Jim Auchmutey and Susan Puckett) 45
Uncle Oscar 64
University of Texas 10, 11
"Upstairs Store, The" 3, 6, 14, 19, passim
U.S. Corps of Engineers 9

"Value Meals" 114–15
Vanilla Ice Cream 166
Vegetables 82–113
  Vegetable Pastalaya 125–26
  Vegetable Seasoning 39
  Vegetable Soup 58–59
  Vegetable Stock 33, 36
Vegetarian Jambalaya 112–13
Vinegar and Oil Dressing 44
Virginia's Cafe 88
Vogue 14
Vulcan Gas Company 12

"Watermelon Dream" (Guy Clark) 148
Wednesday Night Sittin', Singin' and Supper Sessions x, 2, 10, 14
Whipped Cream 164–65
Whole Wheat Bread 79
Wilson, Beulah v, 7, 9, 10, 14, 24, passim
Wilson, Burton 2
Wilson, Eddie ix, passim
Wilson, Sandra 3, 25, passim
Wilson, Woody 10, 25, 72, 88, 170
Wilson's Day Nursery School 10, 86–87, 237

Yams. *See* Sweet Potatoes
Yeast Rolls 77–78
Yellow Squash 107–8
  San Antonio Squash Casserole 109

Zappa, Frank 13